Who the Hell is Abraham Maslow?

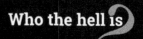

Who the hell is ?

For students, teachers and curious minds, our **carefully structured jargon-free series** helps you really get to grips with brilliant intellectuals and their inherently complex theories.

Written in an **accessible and engaging** way, each book takes you through the **life and influences** of these brilliant intellectuals, before taking a deep dive into three of their **key theories in plain English**.

Smart thinking made easy!

POLITICS   PSYCHOLOGY   PHILOSOPHY   SOCIOLOGY   ART HISTORY

Who the Hell is Abraham Maslow?

And what are his theories all about?

Elizabeth Banks

BOWDEN
&BRAZIL

First published in Great Britain in 2022 by
Bowden & Brazil Ltd
Felixstowe, Suffolk, UK.

British Library Cataloguing-in-Publication Data
A CIP record for this book is available from The British Library.

Academic advisor: Dr. Stuart Lipscombe, University of Suffolk.

ISBN 978-1-915177-00-1

To find out more about other books and authors in this series, visit www.whothehellis.co.uk

Contents

Introduction

'One day just after Pearl Harbor...my car was stopped by a poor, pathetic parade. Boy Scouts and old uniforms and a flag and someone playing a flute off-key. As I watched, the tears began to run down my face. I felt we didn't understand – not Hitler, nor the Germans, nor Stalin, nor the Communists... I felt that if we could understand, then we could make progress. I had a vision of a peace table, with people sitting around it, talking about human nature and hatred, war and peace, and brotherhood... It was at that moment I realized that the rest of my life must be devoted to discovering a psychology for the peace table... Since that moment in 1941, I've devoted myself to developing a theory of human nature that could be tested by experiment and research. I wanted to prove that humans are capable of something grander than war, prejudice, and hatred.'
(Maslow, 1968)

After the horrors of WWII, Abraham Maslow developed an overwhelming sadness for humanity which catalyzed his most powerful works on his theory of motivation, and later on self-actualization, peak experiences, and self-transcendence needs, all of which will be covered throughout this book. One of the most eminent psychologists of the 20th century, Maslow's contribution to psychology is undeniable. His illustrious career spanned some 40 years during which he published almost 30 journal articles, more than 10 books and in 1967, received the honour of 'Humanist of the Year' by the American Humanist Association. But, as we shall see, despite the pervasive anti-Semitism thwarting much of his career, Maslow fought tirelessly for the intelligentsia to recognize humans' innate propensity towards uniqueness, goodness and beauty; values he believed essential to the concept of being 'fully human'. Both radical and innovative, his methods of expanding psychology into first humanism and later transcendence, leave Maslow's ideas far from obsolete. His theories have resonated powerfully and his best-known books, *Motivation and Personality* (1954) and *Toward a Psychology of Being* (1962) continue to guide the fields of psychotherapy, business management, education and theology; his hopes for a united brotherhood remain visible today in people of all races and genders protesting prejudice and gender-focused violence across the globe. Incredibly, beyond the iconic pyramid of needs (which ironically was not even his brainchild), Maslow remains largely uncelebrated by name alone.

Perhaps due to the neglect of his later theories, Maslow's intentions are often misinterpreted and his nemeses Sigmund Freud (1856–1939) and B.F. Skinner (1904–90) continued to dominate. Though scientific, Maslow's biggest gripe with psychodynamics (the idea that unconscious motives and unresolved needs from childhood determine our behaviour and emotions) and behaviourism (the argument that human behaviour can be shaped by the environment using forms of conditioning) was that they were not value-laden and so contributed little to help resolve societal issues, including the institutional racism and inequality that overshadowed most of his career; issues that remain highly relevant today.

The evocative content of Maslow's diaries leave only the stony-hearted indifferent to his desperate need for love and acceptance – needs that undoubtedly impacted both his theories and the people he gravitated towards throughout his life. Sensationally paradoxical, Maslow teetered between great displays of courage and hiding his genius for fear of ridicule. Inveigled by flattery, accusations of a messiah complex would have been music to his ears had he not been timorous of others' dismissive attitudes. But, his bullish nature and unapologetic questioning of psychology's 'greats' was not well received and many important relationships ended leaving him wretched and confused. Sadly, Maslow appeared to be his own worst enemy. Loving fiercely, but conditionally, many – not least his mother – became the unrelenting object of his scathing criticism for failing to meet his high expectations of humans' potential.

A note taker and list maker, his intellectual objective was seldom explicit and, ever evolving, his speeches and writings appear uncultivated and his outlook elusive. The purpose of this book then, is to provide an accessible introduction to Maslow's most precious ideologies for the future of humanity. Unpretentious in style, a propensity towards exaggeration and hyperbole, and an apparent fascination with sex and nudity, we hope that you agree he makes for compelling reading.

1. Maslow's Life Story

Born on 1 April 1908 in Brooklyn, New York, Abraham Harold Maslow was the eldest of seven children born to first-generation Jewish immigrants from Kiev, then part of the Russian Empire (now Ukraine), Samuel Maslow and his first cousin, Rose Schilofsky.

During one of the largest migrations in history, Samuel escaped the imminent threat of the pogroms by emigrating to America. Aged just 14, any uncertainty of what lay ahead was no deterrent compared to the danger of staying; tacitly encouraged by the Czar, the pogroms employed violence and rape to slaughter or persecute ethnic groups, particularly Jews like Samuel. With a dream of financial and political freedom, Samuel set sail. Speaking only Russian and Yiddish, Samuel integrated into his new life by mastering the English language and occupying himself with odd jobs before settling with relatives in New York where he learned to build and repair barrels. It was here that he met, and married, Rose. Shortly afterwards, Abraham was born. Known as Abe, he was followed by six more siblings at roughly two-yearly intervals; Harold, then Paul, Ruth, Sylvia, Lewis and finally Edith, who sadly died in 1926, just two years after her birth.

Parental Cruelty

Working hard to support his growing family, Samuel was often absent from home, making it difficult for Abe to forge any meaningful relationship with him. Instead, he grew afraid of this 'vigorous man, who loved whiskey and women and fighting' (Maslow quoted in Wilson, 1972). When he was present, Samuel was indifferent not only towards his children, but Rose too. The situation between husband and wife worsened over time and any communication turned from subtle indifference to conspicuous anger. Samuel's absences became more tangible and, with the addition of periodic 'business' trips, lasted for longer periods of time. To a young clingy Abe, his father's selfish and irresponsible behaviour substantiated his fears that he was unloved.

Samuel could also be deliberately hurtful towards Abe, once publicly calling him 'ugly' leaving his young son feeling humiliated and ultimately resentful towards his father. During adolescence, such acute feelings of distress coupled with his skinny physique and disproportionately large nose, intensified to the stage that Abe would seek out empty rail carriages to spare others the horror of having to look at him.

While positive memories, including weekend trips for baked apples, were not in the forefront of Abe's mind during such recollections, they did help reconcile him with his father later in life. However, he had no fond memories of his mother whatsoever. Although there is little biological information related to Rose beyond her devoutly religious upbringing, what we do know from Abe is that like her husband, she was neither loving, nor caring towards her children. But, unlike Samuel, her meanness went beyond name-calling; it was chillingly creative and bizarre in its execution. On one occasion, Abe recalls buying a collection of vintage 78-rpm records he had found. On arriving home, however, he forgot to tidy them away. His punishment was witnessing Rose deliberately smashing the records into pieces on the floor where he had left them. Another time, Abe brought home some stray kittens, only to endure the horror of Rose smashing their brains out against a wall because he had fed them using her good saucers.

Regardless of any genetic predispositions or exposure to negativity or threat during his formative years, Abe was a sensitive and empathetic child. But Rose's cruelty left emotional scars that were unquestionably instrumental in Abe's loathing of her and which he unapologetically admitted never diminished over time. To Abe, Rose's sadistic and negligent behaviour caused his little sister Edith's untimely death. At just 16 years of age this was a devastating loss which hit Abe hard, and doubtlessly the catalyst to later arguments that the right to bear children should be considered the utmost social privilege as opposed to any absolute right.

Perhaps due to her alleged egocentrism, Rose seemed blissfully unaware of Abe's feelings towards her. Following tradition, when Abe reached the age of 13, a Bar Mitzvah was arranged as part of his coming of age. Viewing religion, particularly Orthodox Judaism, as totally nonsensical, Abe found the hypocrisy intolerable. Forced to read in a language that he didn't understand, he was also required to pay homage to his parents for their devotion, giving particular thanks to Rose for the gift of life. This righteous display proved insuperable and as Abe ran sobbing, Rose naively declared his inability to express the words as the result of his overwhelming love for her.

Beyond the Barricades

Adopting the survivalist strategy of his father, Abe began avoiding home to escape his mother's wrath. But finding a haven in the Brooklyn Public Library came with its own set of dangers. In the 1920s, New York was a hotbed of anti-Semitism. Due to perceived differences in social and political status between the millions of people looking for work or seeking to escape religious persecution in their homelands, immigrants settled into distinct ethnic or religious enclaves, or blocks, stoking Americans' objections regarding the lack of effort taken to integrate into wider society. Such discordant attitudes were deeply ingrained in the children too and, although recollections from friends and family vary here, Abe vividly remembers being confronted by rival gangs ready and willing to engage in 'warfare' to protect their turf against outsiders. Consequently, navigating a safe route to the library required careful consideration once outside Jewish territory.

Adopting the belief that the most defining characteristic of a real man was physical strength, Abe began weightlifting. However, much to his chagrin, he remained physically delicate throughout his life. While Abe's difficult childhood left him feeling physically vulnerable, socially isolated and lonely, it fuelled his desire to understand the hostility displayed by anti-Semites. Ultimately, this curiosity contributed to one of many factors that led Abe into the field of psychology.

Although derisive of the Jewish religion, Abe always appreciated the emphasis that his Jewish heritage placed upon education; as such, the desire to read and to learn was expected as a matter of course. A voracious reader, early signs of intellectual giftedness

Fig. 1 Brooklyn Public Library, New York.

affirmed Abe's worth; as the eldest son, his parents' expectations of him were especially high. Yet, his success at high school could be described as mediocre at best and many tempestuous years would pass before Abe would show his potential.

Abe's cousin, Will Maslow (1907–2007), was a constant figure throughout his life and one of the first people able to challenge him academically. Later known as the 'Gold Dust' twins, they were inseparable. Through Will, Abe enjoyed an uncharacteristic sense of comradeship and acceptance amongst Will's peers at the prestigious Boys High School in Bedford-Stuyvesant, Brooklyn. Predominantly attended by first-generation American Jews – children, like Abe and Will, of unskilled or semi-skilled immigrants from Europe – these students valued education as the means to prosperity and they provided the much sought-after stimulation Abe craved. Besides holding membership to the chess team and the honour society, Arista, Abe discovered a love for physics and became so excited by Bertrand Russell's (1872–1970) *ABC of Atoms* (1923) that, aged just 15, he wrote an article predicting the possible use of atomic power for submarines and ships, which appeared in the school's academic publication *Principia*, of which he subsequently became editor. Regarding literature, Maslow was indiscriminate, reading everything at his disposal. One recommendation made by his physics teacher, Sebastian Littauer, was so consequential that, eight years later, Abe pinpointed Upton Sinclair's (1878–1968) *Mammonart: An Essay on Economic Interpretation* (1925) as the time his intellectual life began. *Mammonart*, described by Littauer as 'more absorbing' than his current reads, kindled Abe's societal and moral interests and, reading everything that Sinclair had ever written, his democratic socialist principles were born. Although Stalinism would later cure him of his infatuation, socialist leaders including Eugene Debs (1855–1926) and Norman Thomas (1884–1968) became his heroes and he devoured anything he could find related to democratic, utopian ideologies, vowing himself a lifetime of striving for a better world.

Soon the time came to apply for scholarships at the prestigious Cornell University in Ithaca, New York State. But, despite his professed academic superiority, Abe obtained less than outstanding grades in all subjects. Consequently, he decided that any university application would prove futile. Failing to live up to his parents' expectations, circa 1925, Abe applied to the public City College, New York. That Will was successful in securing the scholarship to Cornell was bitter-sweet and, though thrilled for him, Abe was sad knowing that their paths would soon diverge.

The Age of Change

Abe's one saving grace was the blossoming romance between himself and his first cousin, Bertha Goodman. Arriving from Russia in March 1922 at the age of 13, Bertha was a beauty and would later influence Abe's theory on 'peak experiences' – euphoric moments of pure joy – covered in more detail in Chapter 5. Captivated, Abe offered to teach Bertha English, and his weekly visits led to a serious romance that neither could ignore. He grew optimistic about his academic future, but it wasn't long before Abe displayed what would become a long-standing attitude to education: when confronted with subjects that he disliked, for example trigonometry (a prerequisite for his BSc), he disregarded them completely. Unsurprisingly, Abe failed the course. Regardless, he was so convinced of his intellectual greatness that he wrote in his diary, 'my career through high school was distinguished and now in college promises to be brilliant' (Maslow, 1979). Delusional sentiments perhaps from one who found himself on academic probation throughout his second semester.

Yet, despite Abe's initially poor performance having notably improved by the end of his freshman year, Samuel argued that Abe's life as a scholar looked uncertain and railroaded him into pursuing law. Perhaps desperate for approval, Abe dropped all but two full-credit courses to manage this additional burden which he did on a part-time basis at night school. After just two months, however, he decided that law was dry and boring and dealt exclusively with evil and the sins of mankind and subsequently, he quit. Noting a general lack of intellectual vivification at City College, he applied to Cornell's state-funded

Fig. 2 Abe's cousin, Will Maslow, c.1940.

College of Agriculture. Without the scholarship, this seemed the ideal way of attending Cornell at minimal cost and with the option of attending as many free liberal arts classes as possible.

Abe's first taste of relative freedom was sweet. In 1927, now aged 19, Abe was reunited with Will and so was provided temporary distraction from his passionate thoughts about Bertha; a self-proclaimed 'powerfully sexed' being, he was growing increasingly frustrated with the lack of physical intimacy in their relationship and welcomed the mental intrusion. However, faced with navigating the pervasive anti-Semitism manifesting from peers who he determined as intellectually inferior, Abe became disillusioned. Overt racial discrimination flourished at Cornell and all minority groups, including Jews, were effectively barred from rooming houses, fraternities and sororities and even staff positions on student newspapers. Renouncing the conceited, competitive university after just one semester, Abe returned to New York.

Liberation Through Education

Arriving back at City College, Abe discovered a penchant for Beethoven's romanticism and the realism of Eugene O'Neill (1888–1953) plays. It was also around this time that his attraction to anthropology and the notion of cross-cultural variability was ignited after reading the book *Folkways* (1906), by social scientist William Graham Sumner (1840–1910), which he described as a 'Mount Everest' in his life. Based upon social Darwinism and the belief that, in every generation, a few superior individuals (like Abe), were responsible for carrying the dead weight of the shallow, narrow-minded and prejudiced masses (like his mother Rose), he was riveted. Lingering over the 'most savage customs of the most savage people', *Folkways* was so powerful that Abe felt that Sumner was speaking directly to him. Reminded of his earlier commitment to create a better world, Abe was now more determined than ever. But, beyond this initial ambition, it would take another five years or so for a full revelation to occur. Around 1936, after an informal introduction to anthropologist Ruth Benedict (1887–1948) by Ralph Linton, professor of anthropology at the University of Wisconsin-Madison, Abe declared himself a part-time anthropologist, which he believed to be indispensable if one wanted to become a good psychologist. Otherwise, he maintained, you would be no different from any other 'naive local'. We will look at how Benedict's cultural relativism influenced Maslow and his first foray into anthropological fieldwork in greater detail in the next chapter.

In the spring of 1928, Abe's decision to study at the University of Wisconsin-Madison brought with it a period of relative stability. Although still naive in terms of what formal education could offer, his mediocre grades became a thing of the past and his achievements showed uniform excellence. Accredited by the National Honor Society for academic merit, Abe was recognized for his genius and, naturally, he flourished. He remained at Wisconsin-Madison for the following seven years, completing his BA in 1930, his MSc in 1931 and his PhD in 1934, the latter under the supervision of the psychologist Harry Harlow (1905–1981) whose influence we will look at in more detail in Chapter 2. Although happy with his academic commitments and busy fulfilling his role as teaching assistant to psychologists William H. Sheldon (1898–1977), and then Richard W. Husband (1904–1995), Abe missed Bertha immensely. Desperate to make their love affair permanent, on New Year's Eve 1929, Abe married the only woman he would ever know romantically. The emotional security of being loved suited Abe and he thrived. In his article 'Farther Reaches of Human Nature' (1971), he spoke about his marriage as:

> *'Certainly far more important than my PhD by way of instructiveness. If one thinks in terms of developing the kind of wisdom, the kinds of understanding, the kinds of life skills that we would want, then he must think in terms of what I would like to call intrinsic education— intrinsic learning: that is learning to be a human being in general, and second, learning to be this human being.'*

The year 1929 saw the emergence of the Great Depression. Americans began questioning their government and the city of Madison welcomed a culture of left-wing radicalism. The Maslows became part of a cooperative living arrangement which was dedicated to the common goal of shunning capitalism and, loving this affordable style of living, the newlyweds revelled in the close friendships that blossomed. Forthright, Abe enjoyed spirited discussion but his involvement with the socialist party typically went no further than verbal discourse; that is, until 1931 when his teaching salary was threatened as part of a money saving effort by the Wisconsin legislature. Even then, Abe wasn't – and never would be – an activist and avoided deeper involvement other than signing the petition that ultimately saved his job. Still, the threat of losing his income roused feelings of concern regarding his Jewish background and the subtle, if not insidious, anti-Semitism infiltrating Wisconsin-Madison academia. Tired of ignorant, exclusive behaviour, Abe was appalled at his peers' suggestion that he change his name to something less ethnic. With Bertha's grave threat of divorce if he did, Abe adamantly refused, threatening to stuff his Jewishness down anyone's throats if they had a problem with it.

After earning his doctorate, Abe faced the harsh reality of finding employment. As colleagues had warned, despite his impressive credentials, attempts to transition into the workforce were difficult. The nepotism of the 'old boys club' did not extend to him and he had no choice but to enrol in medical school. Unsurprisingly, this was a bad fit and he quit within the year. Relying entirely on his part-time teaching, 1935 was emotionally and financially draining on the young couple. Mercifully, with the help of his friend and colleague, psychologist Gardner Murphy (1895–1979), Abe secured a year-long postdoctoral position as scientific assistant to lionised psychologist Edward Thorndike (1874–1949) at the Institute of Educational Research, Columbia University, beginning that summer. Just a few years after the very worst of the Great Depression, and with his Jewish name intact, this position was quite an accomplishment. Though the hiring of a Jew came with its own risks, Thorndike had been so impressed with Abe's score of 195 on his IQ test two years before that he vowed to support him for the rest of his life if he was unsuccessful in finding a permanent position when their time together came to an end. But, though initially ecstatic at the opportunity to work with Thorndike on his *Human Nature and the Social Order* (1940), within months Abe was bored and arrogantly claimed Thorndike's theory to be misguided and idealistic. Remarkably, Thorndike applauded his reasoning and offered Abe absolute intellectual freedom from that point on.

The Brooklyn Years

Employment for Jews remained uncertain but Abe's 'angel', Thorndike, secured a position for him at Brooklyn College – the first public coeducational liberal arts college in New York City – where he stayed from 1937 to 1951. While his teaching commitment was brutal, Abe enjoyed educating the cohort comprising ambitious, hard-working children of immigrants and, in turn, they held him in high esteem. Warm, engaging and sophisticated, he was known as the 'Frank Sinatra of Brooklyn College' (Frager, 1987a). Given the self-loathing he expressed towards his appearance as a young boy, this was unchartered territory and Abe revelled in the attention. His reputation saw him promoted within his first year from 'tutor' to 'instructor'. But, even with the publication of *Principles of Abnormal Psychology* (1941) under his belt – a prerequisite for tenure or promotion – it would be a long, frustrating wait before Abe's rise to assistant professor would come about. Impatient, he became disheartened. This, in turn, took its toll on his health which had been failing him for quite some time.

In January of 1938, Abe's daughter Ann was born, followed two years later by her sister, Ellen. The Maslow household was one of warmth and love. Enchanted by his daughters and their idiosyncrasies, apparent even before birth, Abe questioned all that he believed true about human nature. Looking back at becoming a father for the first time, he writes: 'I looked at this tiny, mysterious thing and felt so stupid. I was stunned by the mystery and by the sense of not really being in control [...] I'd say that anyone who had a baby couldn't be a behaviorist' (Maslow, 1968b).

Having returned to a communal living arrangement, the first eight years of the girls' lives were spent living amongst various extended family members. Although they all enjoyed each other's company and were fully committed to their fair share of household chores, all financial responsibilities fell solely on Abe driving him to maintain various part-time teaching jobs besides his full-time commitments. Yet, Abe reminisced with great fondness that, while they owned nothing outright, everyone enjoyed a good quality of life, including the intimacy and warmth of the group. The only blot on their horizon was the steady rise of fascism in Europe and, following the attack on Pearl Harbour on 7 December 1941, America formally entered WWII.

It was around this time that left-wing radicalism began permeating Columbia University and not long afterwards it reached Brooklyn College. Through *The Staff*, an anonymous publication, Brooklyn College became known as the 'Little Red Schoolhouse' due to demands that all faculty follow the communist party line. As a democratic socialist, Abe was unsettled. Stalinism infiltrated its way onto the college campus and the once-stimulating environment began reflecting the tumultuous atmosphere felt in the wider community. Largely inhabited by poor and lower-class migrants with little to lose by embracing such radical change, the movement gained momentum. Whereas before Abe was afforded the luxury of internalizing his opinions, now his indifference was challenged and he felt bitterness from both sides demanding that he choose between them. Although capitalism gained some respect with the allegiance of America and the Soviet Union in WWII, Abe never forgot his colleagues' naive contempt for the individual freedoms he believed to be America's greatest asset.

Disturbing Diagnosis

Despite Abe's socialist beliefs and his commitment to a cooperative way of life, financially he continued to struggle. His sister Ruth was enjoying a comfortable lifestyle collaborating with her husband, renowned anthropologist Oscar Lewis (1914–1970), and his brothers were financially secure due to their involvement in Samuel's cooperage business. Nevertheless, despite department politics and Bertha's frequent reminders that his job was a financial dead end, Abe loved teaching at Brooklyn College and firmly declined his brothers' frequent offers of employment. Come 1946, however, Abe could no longer ignore the unrelenting fatigue he had been suffering over the past few years. Though never celebrated for his physical stamina, aged just 38, Abe's unnerving need to nap between lectures did not go unnoticed. His lack of energy was so debilitating that, with trepidation, he sought medical help. Diagnosed with a probable malignant tumour, Abe was forced to face his own mortality. Utterly devastated at the thought of not seeing Ann and Ellen grow, alongside the prospect of leaving Bertha a widow, Abe also mourned what seemed like the death of his life's work on bringing morals and values into psychological research. Stoically, he made his will and prepared to die.

That Abe remained weak was undeniable but, as time passed, his brothers grew sceptical about his diagnosis. Affording him the opportunity of providing for his family at a slower pace of life, Abe finally surrendered to his brothers' offer and, beginning 2 February 1947, he took a medical leave of absence from Brooklyn College and the family set off for rural Pleasanton, California. Although Abe would grossly exaggerate his responsibilities at the Maslow Cooperage Corporation in years to come, referring to himself as 'plant manager', the experience was pivotal in his later theories on management. Within months he had regained his former energy and was ready to rejoin the Brooklyn set.

Brandeis' Bond

By 1951, Abe's hard work was gaining recognition, particularly by Brandeis University in Boston, Massachusetts, where he was offered the respected position of professor. Founded in 1948 as a non-sectarian, coeducational institution sponsored by the Jewish community, Brandeis promised carte blanche in an environment free from the political restraints still imposed upon Jews. Desperate to avoid the infighting and divisiveness experienced throughout his tenure at Brooklyn College, Abe chose his young, energetic faculty carefully. During its evolution though, he realized the arduous task he had undertaken and resignedly packed away his own academic research and personal writing that he had been undertaking.

Initially Abe was liked and respected by his colleagues and he savoured their affection and friendship. Intelligent and witty, Abe used corrective humour and utilised double-entendres skillfully, holding everyone captivated for hours. However, his popularity was to be short-lived. Abe's idealism was considered naïve by some of his colleagues, and his bullish way of penetrating their conversations about their own disciplines, which he knew surprisingly little about, irritated them to the point of disregarding his contributions completely. Accused of acquiring a messiah complex – a compulsion to redeem or save others – Abe's somewhat delusional belief in himself as 'saviour' evolved into intellectual prejudices at Brandeis, resulting in his colleagues losing sight of the potential importance of his work. Cognizant of others' opinions of him and his work, Maslow is quoted as saying, 'I have no real colleagues in the Boston area. My closest one is Frank Manuel, with whom I have good debates, and he thinks my work is a lot of shit' (Maslow quoted in Hoffman, 1999).

Alas so, it seemed, did his students. Unlike those at Brooklyn College who paid Abe the same filial respect he had shown his own mentors, students at Brandeis were more likely to avoid his class than to attend it. Refusing to accept responsibility, he attributed these failed relationships to his students' personal weaknesses in terms of academic performance. Believing them to be self-indulgent and intellectually undisciplined, not to mention lacking in ambition, Abe often wished that everyone but the most capable would drop out so that pioneers like himself could work untroubled by their needy intrusions; students are in plentiful supply, he often thought, whereas discoverers like himself were not. Unsurprisingly, familiar feelings of exploitation and resentment brewed and, once again, Abe found himself wondering why he couldn't leave Brandeis.

But six gruelling years in, while proud of the department he had built, Abe was more than ready for a sabbatical. In the summer of 1957, everyone except Ellen drove cross country visiting family and friends en route to their chosen destination: Cuernavaca, Mexico. Bertha was excited about immersing herself in the Spanish culture, while Ann eagerly anticipated studying art as part of a junior-year-abroad programme. Abe spent hours, just as he had as a child, lost in solitary reading; now though, he was by his pool and had no external commitments to disrupt the creative energy he had long since abandoned. Although not as productive as he had hoped, Abe was in 'heaven'. After a few months of glorious seclusion, he drove to Mexico City to attend a luncheon address on 'Culture, Family values, and Psychotherapy' presented by psychologist Rogelio Díaz-Guerrero (1918–2004). On meeting, the two men fell into an effortless friendship that included lively discussions on Abe's theory of self-actualization – an innate need, or desire, to realize or fulfil one's potentialities (see Chapter 4) – and Díaz-Guerrero's belief that actualization, though possible for anyone to achieve, would manifest itself differently from one culture to another. We will look at Díaz-Guerrero's influence on Maslow and his interest in anthropology in more detail in the next chapter.

Fourteen months later, Abe planned his return to Brandeis, eager to critique science's value-free ideology. But as head of department his role involved time-consuming responsibilities.

Embittered, he now realized that time was short and allowing anything, or anyone, to get in the way of publishing his 'great message' before he died, would be senseless.

Political Turmoil

It was inevitable that over time history would repeat itself. By 1960, the cultural sphere of the civil rights movement had polarized into two competing factions; the war in Vietnam was raging and Americans' faith in their politicians' ability to deal with issues both domestic and abroad plummeted to levels not seen since the Great Depression. Progressively distancing himself from campus affairs, Abe left the American Civil Liberties Union and resigned as a board member of SANE (Committee for a Sane Nuclear Policy), no longer believing that either group had a realistic grasp of human aggression or how to deal with it. Falling into conflict with the popular political view at the time, he became disillusioned and unsettled, feeling even more isolated and alone amongst his colleagues. Highlighting the depths of his anger and despondency, one diary entry reads:

> *'The university world can now, I think, be essentially characterized as value-confused, value-mistrusting, counter-valuing, value-hating. They don't know right from wrong and maybe don't even believe it's possible, or that there are such things.' (Maslow, 1979)*

It was around this time that Abe grew increasingly interested in 'aggridants', or dominant personalities. His relationship with his daughter Ellen, a New Left activist, became strained with Abe arguing that her social outlook was too simplistic. While extremely proud of Ellen's participation in fighting for Blacks' right to vote years before, he grew increasingly impatient with her differing viewpoint which Abe believed was non-ideological and anti-intellectual. He was tortured by her reluctance to believe that, regardless of race or class, America afforded individuals the opportunity to become whatever they choose. He considered the activists to be rejecting society and warned Ellen that unless they compromised, they were all doomed to disillusionment. Weary, Abe was ready for another sabbatical, but Brandeis' approval came with caveats. Enraged at being asked to defer until June of the following year, 1961, and granted just one semester off rather than the two requested, Abe almost quit. But, having lived through the Depression, he knew how forced hardship might affect his relationship with Bertha. Financially bound, Abe had no choice but to acquiesce.

The Twilight Years

Over the next few years Abe's theories on motivation and personality began making an unexpected transition into the realm of business management. In 1962, after a stint observing real-life testing of his theories at Non-Linear Systems (NLS), an electronics manufacturing company based in San Diego, California, he was excited to find that the experiment was leading to reduced absenteeism and increased productivity. His observations were published in 1965 as *Eupsychian Management* (eupsychian being the move towards a psychologically healthy or self-actualized society or organization) bringing Abe international acclaim from enlightened managers sold on humanizing the workplace.

Sadly, Abe's health deteriorated markedly. Due to scarring of his heart tissue, doctors revealed that his earlier diagnosis was more likely the result of a heart attack than a tumour and advised him to live cautiously. Though lamenting this disappointing news, the birth of his first grandchild in 1968 revived Abe's spirits. Still fatigued, and with the fragility of his heart looming ominously, Ann's daughter Jeannie invoked in him the will to live long enough to see her grow; her arrival reinforcing that it was time to quit teaching.

Fortuitously, that same year (1968) *Eupsychian Management* caught the attention of William Laughlin, wealthy co-founder of the Saga Administration Corporation, a food services company based in Menlo Park, California. Hugely impressed with Abe's theories on enlightened management, Laughlin presented him with an unprecedented opportunity: a two-to-four-year commitment to focus on absolutely nothing but his research. Desperately unhappy at Brandeis, Laughlin's offer of a handsome salary, car, secretary and private office left Abe wondering whether it was too good to be true. But any doubts were soon dispelled by the deliberate vandalism of students' theses by black students protesting against perceived racism at the university. Regardless of their reasons, Abe was disgusted with both the protagonists' behaviour and the timidity of Brandeis in terms of their response. Leaving such childish nonsense behind, he gratefully accepted Laughlin's offer and never looked back, enjoying the last years of his life fulfilling his prophecy of becoming the next great saviour.

After his parents' inevitable divorce in the early 1930s, Abe was reconciled with his father. Having lost his business and savings during the Depression, Samuel lived with the Maslows and their extended family members in their co-op. Father and son grew fond of each other over time but, even after years of psychoanalysis (an interesting choice of therapy perhaps given his criticism of this approach) Abe could never bring himself to forgive, nor forget, Rose's disturbing behaviours. Remaining estranged from her throughout her life created much perturbation for his siblings who could not corroborate Abe's painful memories of their childhood. Sadly, aside from one tense meeting at his daughter Ellen's wedding, he never saw his mother again. With no thought of Rose being the victim of her own upbringing or unhappy marriage, his resentment lasted until her death when, showing neither grace nor mercy, Abe steadfastly refused to attend her funeral.

Plagued with heart issues throughout his adult life, Abe died on 8 June 1970 while exercising at the instruction of his doctor. He was just 62 years of age and in the midst of a hugely productive career. With 'at least two hundred years' worth' of work left to accomplish, Abe's legacy of making the world a better place lived on in his two daughters, Ann and Ellen, whose acts of service to their respective communities spanned decades. Fellow humanitarians, both women fought tirelessly for the rights of marginalized groups. Like her father, Ellen died in her sixties after developing breast cancer. Like Bertha, Ann lived until the age of 82. Sadly, in April 2020, she contracted Covid-19 which ultimately claimed her life.

Abraham Maslow's Timeline

Abraham Maslow	World Events
	1897 Birth of psychoanalysis
1908 Abraham Harold Maslow is born, Brooklyn, New York	
	1909 Civil rights organization, NAACP, is formed
	1910 Roosevelt gives New Nationalism speech
	1912 Birth of Gestalt psychology
	1913 Birth of Behaviourism
	1914 -18 WW1
	1917 America enters WW1
	1920 Women gain the right to vote in the USA
1921 Becomes bar mitzvah at age 13	
1922 Attends Boys High School, Bedford-Stuyvesant, Brooklyn; Cousin Bertha arrives in USA	**1922** Fascist leader Mussolini seizes power in Italy
1923 First article published in school's academic publication, *Principia*	
1925 Interest in Socialism is ignited; Enrols in City College, New York	
1927 Enrols at Cornell School of Agriculture; Re-enrols at City College, New York	
1928 University of Wisconsin-Madison; Marries Bertha Goodman	
	1929 Wall Street Crash triggers the Great Depression
1930 Receives BA from Wisconsin-Madison	
1931 MSc research supervized by Harry Harlow; Receives MSc	
1932 Renewed interest in Freudian psychology	**1932** Franklin D. Roosevelt is elected President of the United States
1933 Formal application to NRC, Florida	**1933** Hitler becomes Chancellor of Germany; Socialist Movement begins
1934 Receives PhD from Uni of Wisconsin-Madison; Teaches part-time at Wisconsin-Madison; Enrols at Wisconsin Medical School	
1935 Begins post-doctoral position at Thorndike's Institute of Educational Research	**1935** First Harlem riot takes place
1937 Secures position at Brooklyn College	
1938 Begins research on Blackfoot Native Americans; Daughter Ann is born	**1939** WWII begins; Sigmund Freud dies
1940 Daughter Ellen is born	**1940** America enters WWII; Fight for Freedom Committee founded; America 1st Committee founded

Year		Year	
1941	Publishes *Principles of Abnormal Psychology*	1941	Japan bombs Pearl Harbour
1943	Publishes *A Theory of Human Motivation*		
		1945	WWII ends
1947	Suffers first heart attack	1947	Cold War begins
1948	Takes medical leave of absence; Works with brothers at West Coast Cooperage plant	1948	Executive Order 9981 is issued, abolishing discrimination
1949	Returns to Brooklyn College		
1951	Takes up position of professor at Brandeis University	1950	Start of McCarthyism Start of McCarthyism
1954	*Motivation and Personality* is published; Birth of humanistic psychology		
		1955	Vietnam War begins
1958	Takes sabbatical in Mexico	1958	Harry Harlow publishes *The Nature of Love*
		1960	Rioting in Algiers
1962	Returns to Brandeis; Co-founds Association for Humanistic Psychology; Publishes *Toward a Psychology of Being*	1962	Cuban Missile Crisis
		1963	President Kennedy is assassinated; Betty Friedan publishes *The Feminine Mystique*
1964	Publishes *Religions, Values, and Peak Experiences*	1964	Civil Rights Act and Voting Rights Act passed
1965	Publishes *Eupsychian Management*		
1966	Publishes *The Psychology of Science: A Reconnaissance*		
1967	Awarded 'Humanist of the Year'		
1968	Publishes second edition of *Towards a Psychology of Being*	1968	Student and worker uprisings in France
1969	Fellowship at Saga Administrative Corporation in Menlo Park, California	1969	Stonewall riots in New York City
1970	Revises *Motivation and Personality*; Abraham Maslow dies in Menlo Park, California		
1971	*The Farther Reaches of Human Nature* publishes posthumously; Awarded the American Psychological Foundation Gold Medal Award for Impact in Psychology		

2. Influences on Maslow's Thinking

Having experienced mental cruelty, rejection and prejudice at various points throughout his life, Abraham Maslow set out on a path to address psychological health which eventually led to his hierarchy of needs and his theory on self-actualization. Along the way, he encountered many important thinkers who would alter and influence the direction that this path took. From behaviourism, psychoanalysis and Gestalt psychology to neurology and anthropology, theories from the leading minds in these fields formed the basis from which Maslow would go on to achieve his own theories of psychological health.

At the time that Maslow graduated from Wisconsin-Madison in 1934, John B. Watson's (1878–1958) behaviourism (known as the 'first force') and Freud's psychoanalytic theory (the 'second force') dominated the field. During his early career, Maslow was a great believer in behaviourism and was inspired by the possibilities of building a better society – one that was more tolerant and inclusive than the one he had grown up in. Psychoanalytic theory, too, was initially exciting to Maslow who, at last, had found a theory that came closest to any other in terms of explaining his own experiences in life to date.

As time went on, Maslow would come across many other important names in the field of psychology, including the social-cognitive psychologist Harry Harlow, the founder of Individual psychology Alfred Adler (1870–1937), Gestalt psychologists Kurt Goldstein (1878–1965) and Max Wertheimer (1880–1943), and anthropologists Ruth Benedict and Diaz-Guerrero.

Behaviourism: Watson and Harlow

In preparation for undergraduate study, Maslow read the work of John B. Watson, the founder of behaviourism. Staunchly committed to social change, Watson believed that the only difference between people in terms of potential was the social class they were born into; if you change that, he said, then the possibilities are endless. Watson's work produced 'an explosion of excitement' in Maslow. Watson's notion of studying purely observable behaviour in an objective, scientific way led Maslow to join the psychology graduate program at the University of Wisconsin-Madison where he focused entirely on behaviourism under the supervision of Harry Harlow.

But the behaviourists' notion that attachment is nothing more than a way of securing food from a caregiver by way of operant conditioning and reinforcements overlooked what Harlow saw as an innate (biological) need to be loved. For decades, Harlow pioneered research into infant–mother bonding in primates. He is perhaps best known for his infamous social-isolation experiments using rhesus monkeys conducted between 1957 and 1963, and the notoriously unethical equipment that he himself designed and which he referred to using deliberately unconventional terminology. These included a forced-mating device he called the 'rape rack', metal surrogate-mothers called 'iron maidens', and an isolation chamber known as the 'pit of despair'. Skinnerians would have predicted the monkeys' behaviour to be reinforced through association with the surrogate mother offering rewards of milk. Harlow, though, would effectively demonstrate that baby rhesus monkeys, when given the choice, would choose love and comfort over food, particularly when afraid or distressed. With forces other than the principles of behaviourism clearly guiding the monkeys' response to their environment, Harlow showed just how important love is and that to neglect a monkey's need to be loved leaves it vulnerable to profound psychological and emotional distress. Essentially, Harlow was committed to disproving Watson's notion that 'mother love is a dangerous instrument'.

Maslow conducted his own research on primates between 1933 and 1940, focusing primarily on food preferences, appetites and hunger, and the role of dominance in the social and sexual behaviour of primates. It quickly became apparent that the monkeys' behaviour was driven by different sets of needs and that some of these needs took precedence over others. For example, when given a choice, fulfilling basic needs such as thirst were noticeably more important to them than fulfilling feelings of hunger. From these observations, Maslow deduced that they possessed an innate knowledge about which of the two needs must be fulfilled first in order to stay alive for longer. Simultaneously, Maslow was able to highlight a clear dichotomy between appetite and hunger, debunking the behaviourist explanation of motivation as a drive only to survive. As observed, if animals will eat food that is appealing beyond satiation, but actively reject food that isn't, Maslow argued the need for a more sophisticated explanation than the one proffered by the behaviourists. This pivotal conclusion would foreshadow his highly influential theory of human motivation (see Chapter 3).

Psychoanalysis: Alfred Adler

Around this time, Maslow read Freud's *The Interpretation of Dreams* (1899) and began contemplating whether behaviour motivated by internal biological drives, such as sex and aggression, could explain dominant behaviour in primates or whether, as Freud's erstwhile counterpart Alfred Adler suggested, it was born out of social influence and the striving for mastery and power. Maslow – intrigued by Adler's propositions – was excited about pitting two of psychology's greats against each other and, with Harlow's consent, began his own research into dominance and sexuality in rhesus monkeys for his dissertation. The results of his year-long experiment were irrefutable; a monkey's dominance or power status appeared to determine its expression of sexuality, not the other way around. In short, at least when drawing an analogy to human behaviour, it was Adler, not Freud, who appeared more correct.

Elated, Maslow interpreted his results as a vindication of Adler's Individual psychology over psychoanalysis which, in his mind, had held the reins for too long. Harlow was duly impressed and later commented that Maslow's research was so innovative and the outcome so radical that to have described him as merely 'ahead of his time' would have been a gross understatement of the importance of his contributions to this field – contributions that remained definitive for decades. An invitation to publish a summary of his dissertation in Adler's *International Journal of Individual Psychology* in 1935, led to a frequent sharing of ideas between the two men.

One of many distinguished émigrés seeking a haven at the University in Exile – a self-governing research unit within the New School for Social Research in New York – Adler became one of Maslow's most important mentors and the one to which Maslow admitted owing a great 'intellectual debt'. At one of Adler's Friday night soirees, Maslow was formally introduced to Adler by mutual friend Heinz Ansbacher (1904–2006) – an early follower of classical Adlerian psychology – and the two developed a strong, mutually influential relationship. For the remaining 18 months of Adler's life Maslow revelled in the fatherly attention bestowed upon him.

Like many other European émigrés, Adler started his career as a medical doctor but, after reading *The Interpretation of Dreams*, had switched his focus to psychoanalysis. Co-founder of the development of psychoanalysis and president of the Vienna Psychoanalytic Society, Adler was highly respected as one of the sharpest minds in the entire circle. But although Freud took the content of Adler's views seriously, despite being at odds with his own, he declared them 'misguided'. Well-known for responding harshly to those he saw as dissenters, by 1911, the antagonism between the Freud and Adler became untenable, creating discord and ultimately a division in the Psychoanalytic Society. Adler, and those that supported him – the Adlerians – broke rank and founded the Society of Individual Psychology in 1912, based upon Adler's key belief that humanity has one basic desire and goal: to belong and to feel significant.

Adler's construct of movement, from inadequacy (or inferiority) to adequacy (or superiority), is arguably his biggest influence on Maslow's hierarchy of needs (see Chapter 3). Having played second fiddle to his elder brother in childhood and suffered an illness that resulted in physical limitations and rejection by his peers, Adler concluded that these events would have made him a high risk for developing, what he later called, an 'inferiority complex'. Adler believed that everyone experiences feelings of inferiority at some point in time, leading some people to spiral towards depression, attention-seeking or fierce competitiveness. He considered this to be nothing more than psychological defence mechanisms used to compensate for, or conceal, self-perceived inferiority. Others, he argued, would use feelings of inferiority to move, or strive towards, a 'fictional final goal', or superiority.

Openly passionate about social issues, including discriminatory conditions that fuelled youngsters' feelings of inferiority or inadequacy, Adler argued that reforms in child-rearing methods and education were required if improvements in mental health were to be seen. This emphasis on environmental factors affecting, for example, juvenile delinquency and crime, resonated strongly with Maslow and, while his own theory of motivation was by no means complete, he was certain that the effort required to move from basic needs to the higher levels of self-fulfillment, or self-actualization, involved life-long, goal-orientated effort. According to Ansbacher and Ansbacher (1956), this notion was already in line with Adler's concept of 'striving-to-overcome' – the movement from inadequate to adequate – as the one basic dynamic force behind all human activity.

Unfortunately, Maslow's relationship with Adler was not to last. Maslow's casual suggestion that Adler had been one of Freud's disciples was angrily shut down as both a 'lie and a swindle' and all ties were severed (Adler quoted in Odajnyk, 2012). Regrettably, Adler died of a heart attack just 18 months later in 1937 before any reconciliation had taken place, leaving Maslow emotionally shattered. But, despite any differences in terms of their thinking, Adler's influence on Maslow was one of great optimism regarding humans' capabilities, given the right circumstances. While the psychological theories of each man are rarely mentioned in conjunction with each other today, the combined effect of Maslow's description of the prospective destination for human potential and Adler's strategies for helping people get there are inspirational. For the remainder of Maslow's career, he drew unwavering attention to Adler and key Adlerian concepts in terms of their significant contributions to the humanistic movement.

Gestalt Psychology: Max Wertheimer

At the time that Adler was establishing Individual psychology, Max Wertheimer was building his own reputation at the University of Frankfurt in Germany on the back of his famous habilitation thesis, published in 1912. In his thesis, he first described the 'Phi Phenomenon', an optical illusion where stationary items, shown in quick succession, exceed the limit at which they can be perceived separately, resulting in apparent – or as he called it the 'impression' of – movement. Together with co-founders Kurt Koffka (1886–1941) and Wolfgang Köhler (1887–1967), this marked the birth of Gestalt psychology (*gestalt* meaning 'pattern' or 'configuration' in German).

To Wertheimer, apparent movement was a natural phenomenon that needed no further clarification; movement exists *exactly* as it is perceived and, as such, it could not be explained more simply. Contrary to the misconception that 'the whole is *greater* than the sum of its parts', Wertheimer argues that 'the whole is typically so *different* from the sum of its parts that thinking in any such summative terms yields only a caricature of genuine reality' (author's italics, Wertheimer, 1965). Simply put, we could never accurately predict a whole based purely on its individual parts. Taking a look at illusory contours such as the Kanizsa Triangle (see Fig. 3), three figures – here it is the old video game character Pac-Man – are strategically placed to suggest that a unilateral triangle existed between them. Objectively, no triangle exists but here the triangle is a gestalt in that it acts as an independent whole affecting your perception, or interpretation, of each individual part of the image. What this means is that if we were to cover two of the figures, we no longer perceive a white corner in a black circle in the remaining image – we see Pac-Man. As such, we must accept that the 'whole' (the triangle, the gestalt) has an *independent* existence in the perceptual system and that it is this whole that influences our perception of the parts, not the other way round. Thus, according to Koffka,

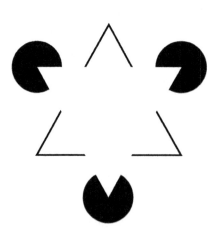

Fig. 3 The Kanizsa Triangle.

it should now be clear to see that 'the whole is something else [different] than the sum of its parts, because summing is a meaningless procedure, whereas the whole–part relationship is meaningful.' (Koffka, 1935)

Seeing whole patterns rather than individual configurations led to what Wertheimer called 'aha'

Fig. 4 The Rubin Vase.

moments. These were moments of sudden insight where the whole or pattern makes absolute sense, rather than looking at individual parts separately, as the behaviourists were wont to do. This helped to determine a new way of understanding that considered the behavioural environment, the cultural context and the ego as a totality. Approaching something from different perspectives alters what we see. Take the Rubin Vase as an example (see Fig. 4). The image presents a choice of *two* mental interpretations: either two faces in the foreground and a vase in the background, or a vase in the foreground and two faces in the background – either of which is valid. After some time or prompting one may experience a 'Gestalt switch' occurring between one interpretation and the other. But you will find that it is impossible to perceive them both simultaneously; one image will always occlude the other. To Wertheimer, Gestalt was not just a theory of thinking and perceiving, but more a *Weltanschauung* – a philosophy of life.

Under Wertheimer, the only psychologist seeking refuge at the New School for Social Research in 1933 (by then in its 14th year), the university became known for its centre for Gestalt psychology. Having heard segments of Hitler's speech on the radio while working at the University of Frankfurt, Wertheimer, like Koffka and Köhler, left for the United States where he spent the remaining 10 years of his life. Wertheimer's introductory psychology lectures became a regular fixture for Maslow and, after their initial meeting in 1935, he quickly became Maslow's most inspiring mentor. Warm, unassuming and encouraging, it was inevitable that Wertheimer would become a much longed-for surrogate father. To Maslow, Wertheimer embodied all the characteristics of what Maslow would later call the 'self-actualizing' person (see Chapter 4).

In *Some Problems in the Theory of Ethics* (1935), Wertheimer challenged science to assume the role and responsibility of diversifying investigations to include the exploration of morality in society. Voicing an optimism shared by Maslow, he declared that overall humanity was good due to the same set of subtle, but universal, ethical values humans share. At some point in life, he explained, people experience moments of awakening – those aha moments – and become aware of their finest qualities; qualities that they had always possessed but had forgotten or lost along the way. Only by studying people at their best, Wertheimer argued, can we understand them at their worst.

Decrying cultural relativism (the practice of understanding any given culture from its own standards of behaviour rather than the standards of another) as outdated, Wertheimer contended that all that distinguishes one person from another are the relative biological, economic, cultural and sociological factors that interfere with one's development, or realization. 'There seem to be layers in men,' Wertheimer said, 'and it is a question of fact what the inner layers of men really are' (Wertheimer, 1935). To ignore their influence or to make generalizations, he warned, was to ignore the interconnectedness between any one person and their own unique life experience – their *Weltanschauung*.

Maslow was convinced that the investigation of morality was of the utmost significance to human existence and thus to any truly comprehensive approach to the mind. This was perhaps Wertheimer's greatest influence on Maslow's thinking on transcendent awakening, particularly regarding what would later be termed 'peak experiences' (see Chapter 5 for more on this topic). Maslow remained indebted to Wertheimer's influence throughout his career, expressing his gratitude in the preface of all his major publications.

Self-actualization: Kurt Goldstein

Maslow met the émigré intellectual Kurt Goldstein in the late 1930s in New York. It was Goldstein who, in his magnus opus, *The Organism: A Holistic Approach to Biology Derived from Pathological Data in Man* first published in 1934, first introduced the concept of self-actualization: the tendency to actualize (as much as possible) the organism's individual capacities in the world. He later used the term to explain the reorganization of a previously healthy person's abilities after experiencing extreme catastrophe or shock.

During WWI, while working at the Neurological Institute in Frankfurt, Goldstein was provided with an unprecedented opportunity to observe how brain-injured war veterans responded to his multidisciplinary treatments. Shying away from traditional localization, his method was phenomenological in that he studied the *entire* brain as it existed – not only as an interrelated part of the rest of the brain and the body, but as a part of the natural environment that surrounds it too – in order to see the bigger picture. According to Goldstein, when a being is damaged by an intense situation that overwhelms its ability to adequately respond, it restructures its parts into a *new* whole, absorbing the wounds in order to survive. In this way, the damaged being is active, regenerating itself with the aim of achieving self-actualization. Such a novel view challenged the prevailing tendency towards reductionism, suggesting instead that a more holistic approach towards humans' behaviour and their potential may be more insightful.

In his 1943 paper 'A Theory of Human Motivation', Maslow introduced Goldstein's concept of self-actualization but used it in a more specific way, that is 'the desire for self-fulfillment, namely the tendency for him [the individual] to become actualized in what he is potentially. This tendency might be phrased as the desire to become more and more what one is, to become everything that one is capable of becoming'. Like Goldstein, Maslow believed that fulfilling a human's basic needs helps that person towards self-actualization. For example, in Goldstein's brain-injured veterans, their need for safety (which figures high up in Maslow's Hierarchy of Needs – see Chapter 3) is of paramount importance in order to stabilize their world. In avoiding the unfamiliar and strange and in creating an environment that is well-ordered and regimented, everything in their world becomes both predictable and dependable making progression towards self-actualization more likely. But, when Maslow later coined the phrase 'self-actualization' on developing his own theory of motivation, Goldstein was aggrieved. Aggravating the situation further, Maslow diverged from Goldstein's proposition regarding when and how self-actualization might emerge as a motivator. To Goldstein, self-actualization can occur at any point in an organism's lifespan, whereas Maslow argued that the effort required to move from the basic needs in his hierarchy to the higher levels of self-fulfillment, or self-actualization, was a life-long endeavour, rather than something that could occur at any moment in time under any given circumstances. In other words, the desire to self-actualize will only emerge as a motivator once all basic needs have been met. Further, in contrast to Goldstein's proposal that any organism has the potential to actualize itself, Maslow argued that self-actualization is not only rare, but unique to the human species.

Still, we are left with little doubt as to the tremendous foundational impact Goldstein's work had on Maslow's career. Not only in spotlighting the scientific community's tendency towards materialism, and the importance of adopting a holistic approach but also on Maslow's most famous concepts of needs and self-actualization as outlined in *The Organism* (1995) where Goldstein writes:

> *'It is better we speak of "needs". The organism has definite potentialities, and because it has them it has the need to actualize or realize them. The fulfillment of these needs represents the self-actualization of the organism.*

Driven by such needs, we are experiencing ourselves as active personalities not, however, passively impelled by drives experienced as conflicting with the personality.'

Anthropology: Ruth Benedict

At the same time that Goldstein's *The Organism* was released into the European market, anthropologist Ruth Benedict published *Patterns of Culture* (1934) in the United States. Hailed as the most influential book in 20th-century anthropology, Benedict's knowledge of cultural relativism was indisputable. It was while working at Columbia as Thorndike's research assistant that Maslow first met Benedict. Always looking for opportunities to study with leading thinkers of his time, Maslow became a permanent fixture at the anthropology department's weekly seminars. Impressed with Benedict's work, Maslow went on to write his own anthropological perspective in his chapter on 'Personality in Patterns of Culture' presented in Ross Stagner's (1909–97) *The Psychology of Personality* (1937).

By now, Maslow was gaining his own prestige as one of few psychologists in America with any relevant knowledge on cross-cultural issues. However, unlike Benedict who had travelled extensively, Maslow had remained very much a naive local. Pointing out that any element of cultural bias Maslow himself might hold could only be shed through direct exposure to other cultures, Benedict encouraged him to extend his research further afield geographically, offering him financial aid from the Social Science Research Council under her sponsorship. For Maslow, Benedict embodied the same characteristics he had admired in Wertheimer; characteristics that would shape his self-actualizing person further down the line, and he knew that to turn down her offer would be idiotic. So, in the summer of 1938, initially reluctant due to the arrival of his first daughter Ann in January that same year, he set off to study dominance and emotional security amongst the Northern Blackfoot Native Americans in Alberta, Canada. Armed with the belief that we must only treat individuals as members of the general human species after treating them as members of a particular cultural group first, he was, however, just weeks away from changing his mind completely.

Maslow arrived armed with a questionnaire he had specifically designed to measure dominance in the Blackfoot peoples. However, it became immediately apparent that the questions were fraught with the cultural bias Benedict had warned of, rendering the test useless when measuring secure people. Questions included 'How do you react to the shy, timid and bashful man?'; as it was the cultural norm within the group for Blackfoot men to show displays of dominance, no such shy, timid or bashful men existed within the tribe. Another question, this time of the Blackfoot women, asked 'How do you feel about being a housewife and mother as a full-time job?'; as this role was in fact the standard (and only) role of Blackfoot women, it was entirely irrelevant, although it did prove to be a great source of amusement to the Blackfoot people. Eventually, after rephrasing certain questions and removing others altogether, cross-cultural validity was found, forcing Maslow to abandon his notion of cultural relativity as erroneous and not conducive to an overall understanding of human nature. In 1954 he wrote:

> *'It would seem that every human being comes at birth into society, not as a lump of clay to be moulded by society, but rather as a structure which society may warp or suppress or build up [...] my Indians were first human beings and secondly, Blackfoot Indians.'*

His revised outlook on cultural relativism remained prominent in psychology for decades. Taking Benedict's advice had turned out to be one of the best decisions Maslow had ever made and, from that experience alone, he was forced to amend his whole theory on dominance behaviour in humans. The realization that people from different cultures share the same drives eventually led to the development of Maslow's Hierarchy of Needs (see Chapter 3). Unexpectedly, in 1947 Benedict ended all communications with Maslow, leaving him devastated. Baffled at yet another rejection, history was to repeat itself and, like Adler, Benedict died the following year before Maslow found closure on what had been an important relationship to him.

Meeting Díaz-Guerrero in Mexico

Maslow's interest in anthropology was further challenged by Rogelio Díaz-Guerrero's cross-cultural perspective during his trip to Mexico (see Chapter 1). With specific reference to the trait of autonomy, Díaz-Guerrero's argument was that, unlike Americans, Mexicans found greater fulfillment through serving others. In fact, he explained, even before children can correctly pronounce their own name, in response to any question asked of them they must always follow their answer with *para servirle*, 'to serve you'.

He also forced Maslow to question how those living in poverty were likely to actualize through their livelihood which served the sole purpose of feeding the family to keep them alive. Maslow's interest was piqued and, in an unpublished paper from 1959, he says: 'If a man is forbidden to Be by his times, apparently he can get some of the effects of Being via yearning, dreaming, fantasying, idealizing, utopianizing [or through] writing [...] or painting or being religious' (Maslow quoted in Hoffman, 1999). In part, thanks to Díaz-Guerrero, Maslow now saw that in transcending the social order as it existed, everyone could express self-actualization, despite how wretched their circumstances may be.

3. The Third Force:
Humanistic Psychology

Disturbed by the ferocity of WWII and the rise in people turning to fascist dictators like Hitler and Stalin for direction, Maslow admitted spending the rest of his career developing a 'psychology for the peace table' – a psychology that willingly embraced humans' highest morals and values. But Maslow feared that no one in the scientific community appeared interested in anything much beyond the winning of the war, neglecting entirely the struggle for universal values which in his eyes – aside from being the whole point of the war – could lead to continued peace afterwards. Disapproving of current scientific practice, which he considered as 'means-centred', Maslow's biggest complaint was that, with perhaps the best of intentions, scientists tended to dedicate too much precious time researching issues only possible by the techniques, or the means, already at their disposal, by asking 'Which problems can I attack with the techniques and equipment I now possess?' (Maslow, 1954) as opposed to focusing on the most crucial issues that needed resolving – even if this meant finding innovative ways of doing so. Consequently, during that period, Maslow argued that not much was being discovered that wasn't already known.

In order to realize his dream for peace, in 1943 Maslow wrote arguably one of the most famous psychology paper ever written, 'A Theory of Human Motivation'. Detailing what Maslow called the Hierarchy of Needs, it is essentially a description of humans' behavioural motivation to fulfill first physiological, and then psychological needs in a hierarchical order. Beginning with the most basic needs for survival, before moving towards the ultimate goal of self-actualization, the hierarchy of needs reveals Maslow's belief that *all* humans possess an innate desire to become everything that they are capable of becoming, given the right circumstances to grow.

Believing himself to be Freudian, behaviouristic, and humanistic, it is unsurprising that Maslow's theory draws upon a myriad of influences, as described in the previous chapter. From his own life experiences and decades of observing the 'best of humanity', coupled with a synthesis of Freud's dynamicism, Adler's notion of movement towards mastery, Wertheimer's gestalt theory and Goldstein's self-actualization, the hierarchy of needs came to fruition. Often criticized for exploiting others' ideas, Maslow never intended to replace or reject existing theories, but to develop a more accurate image of humans that neither overlooked nor downplayed the potentials of our higher nature. He called these potentials 'instinctoid': our essence; who we are at our biological core. Avoiding derailment by social circumstances, he said, would allow for the discovery and development of these potentials, making actualization achievable.

A Theory of Human Motivation

Maslow's research on monkeys proved that, if given a choice, fulfilling their need to drink was noticeably more important to the monkeys than their need to eat (see Chapter 2). Those denied access to water and other basic needs became visibly more aggressive towards other members of their troop. Such observations confirmed Maslow's suspicions that monkeys whose basic needs were met were ultimately more successful in establishing social roles and dominance (self-esteem) than monkeys whose needs were thwarted.

While teaching at Brooklyn College during the 1940s, Maslow found himself acting as a lay psychotherapist in the absence of any formal counselling available to students. While most students sought basic coping mechanisms to deal with stress-related conflicts at home – typically surrounding issues of morals and values – one former student had more serious concerns including irregular periods, insomnia, lack of appetite and a general discontent with life. Having graduated from Brooklyn College the year before, she was forced to abandon her academic career to provide financial support for her family who were facing hard times. Although well paid, the woman's job was unfulfilling and she was struggling to find any meaning or purpose in anything that she did. Discarding his own version of the psychoanalysis he had used with most other students by ignoring any childhood trauma the woman may have experienced, Maslow focused exclusively on her current-day problems. Suspecting that her need to actualize her talents had been frustrated by her responsibility towards her family, Maslow suggested that she continue studying at night after work. Following his advice, the woman appeared relatively symptom-free and much happier upon their next meeting.

Given that Maslow's only exposure to psychoanalysis had been the result of his own therapy over the years, he questioned what aspects of his advice had led to the most successful outcomes. While presuming that failing to fulfil their inner needs was preventing these students from actualizing their potential, Maslow's inkling that people's needs could be grouped into categories – and that some needs were more essential than others – gained momentum. Turning his attention to emotionally healthy people, he was reminded of Benedict and Wertheimer, 'the best specimens of mankind'. They were puzzling to Maslow; everything he understood about human motivation and behaviour just couldn't explain them. From their first meetings in 1935, Maslow's curiosity regarding the 'normal' personality grew and, with increasing frequency, he would wonder what society would be like if everyone were as motivated and self-fulfilled as they were.

Raising a few eyebrows, Maslow dedicated an entire chapter to an unorthodox overview of the normal personality in *Principles of Abnormal Psychology*, a book he had co-authored in 1941 with Hungarian friend and psychiatrist, Béla Mittelmann (1899–1959). The normal personality, he wrote in a section entitled 'The Ideal Personality and Goals', can demonstrate self-esteem, an awareness of oneself, the ability to give and receive love and the capacity to question the morals and values of society. While we may all agree that values including goodness and truth are as important to any functioning society, it would take further development of his theory for Maslow to define exactly what he believed these values to be (see Chapter 5).

In January 1943, the journal *Psychosomatic Medicine* invited Maslow to publish his integrative approach to human motivation as two papers. The first 'A Preface to Human Motivation' outlined 13 basic propositions that Maslow believed to be crucial to any theory of human motivation in order to be considered definitive. The second, published later that same year, being 'A Theory of Human Motivation'. Due to the complexity of his theory, Maslow knew that misinterpretation and further criticism was likely if he did not first acknowledge the basic propositions. This, he hoped, would help people gain a better understanding of his intention. Here is a brief summary of Maslow's 13 conclusions:

1. Individuals must be seen as integrated 'wholes', as it is the whole person who is motivated and thus gratified, not just a part of them. Using the fictitious 'John Smith', Maslow explains that it is John Smith that wants food, not just John Smith's stomach. So, food satisfies John Smith's hunger, not just John Smith's stomach's hunger. The importance here being that when John Smith is hungry, he will be less able to concentrate on the world around him due to his total preoccupation with food. In other words, 'when John Smith is hungry, he is hungry all over; he is different as an individual from what he is at other times'.

2. Hunger is different from other motivations in that it has a known biological base necessary for survival. The same cannot be said for more common motivations such as the desire for new clothes,

a faster car or more followers on Facebook or Instagram – granted, more contemporary examples than Maslow himself might have chosen back in 1943. Still, Mabe et al (2014) found that eating disorders are commonly reported by excessive social media users who fail to chalk up the desired number of 'likes'. While there is a biological explanation for eating purely for hunger's sake (to aid survival), this does not explain the destructive behaviour of choosing not to eat.

3. Maslow believes that motivation theory should focus on the ends (staying with our more contemporary example, the need to be 'liked'), rather than the means to those ends (how people go about earning those likes). He explains that the particular desires that enter our conscious awareness throughout any given day – for example, the need to be liked – are not, in and of themselves, as important as what they represent and what they ultimately mean upon deeper analysis. As such, unconscious motivations must not be ignored.

4. 'Ends in themselves are far more universal than the roads taken to achieve those ends.' More simply put, the fundamental goals of all humans do not differ nearly as much as the cultural variety in the methods taken to achieve those goals. For example, we may all desire respect (esteem) but in one culture that may come as a result of promoting peace in an egalitarian society, whereas others may demand

respect using a more authoritarian leadership style. Given that we are more alike than we are different, Maslow argues that cultural relativity is outdated.

5. Any motivated behaviour must be understood as a way of expressing or serving more than one purpose simultaneously. For example, we often eat for the pure pleasure of it – to satisfy, or whet, our appetite – not just because we are hungry. Likewise, sexual behaviour may unconsciously satisfy an individual's need to feel loved or wanted, rather than serving only as the end goal of sexual gratification in itself. It would be extremely unusual, Maslow explained, for our actions or conscious desires to have but one motivation.

6. We must appreciate practically all 'whole' humans as both motivated and motivating and accept that the motivational state is incessant and constantly fluctuates. For instance, if we are feeling rejected in some way, we would be motivated to alleviate associated feelings of unhappiness by winning back the desired affection. Once this goal has been achieved, the desire no longer exists and there is no motivation to act. Over time, if feelings of rejection reappear, we are motivated once again to take action.

7. Human needs arrange themselves in hierarchies of pre-potency. As humans are 'perpetually wanting animal[s]' – so, rarely satisfied – the appearance of any given need typically rests on prior satisfaction

of another, greater or 'prepotent' need. An example being that once we have satisfied any feelings of rejection, we now start looking towards higher needs such as esteem for gratification. Afterwards, we seek higher needs still. But, as we shall see, no need or drive should be treated in isolation as each one is related to the level of satisfaction, or dissatisfaction, of the others.

8. Maslow warns against creating lists of drives, arguing that lists imply equality in terms of potency and probability of appearance, which is not the case. According to Maslow, the probability of any one desire appearing depends upon the level of satisfaction or dissatisfaction of other more prepotent desires (see 'hierarchy of relative prepotency' below). Second, he explains that listing drives implies an isolation – or mutual exclusiveness – of each one from all others, which there is not.

9. Any classification of motivated behaviour must be hinged upon the stability of end goals rather than the instigating drives or motivations by which these goals are achieved, as these methods are rarely the same. In accepting that the motivational state is continuously fluctuating and typically satisfies more than one basic need simultaneously, the only constant factor in these fluctuating states *is* the end goal.,

10. Motivation theory should be anthropocentric rather than animal centred. It goes without saying

that 'a white rat is not a human being' and yet Maslow (1954) felt the need to reiterate this point given the over reliance on animal experimentation in the field. But, he stressed, if we must use animals in human motivation research, 'let us prefer the monkey to the white rat [...] if only for the simple reason that we human beings are much more like monkeys than we are like white rats'.

11. Any actualized behaviour must be considered in the context of other people *and* the situation in which it occurred, including the role of any cultural determinants. Chapter 1 relayed how Maslow's father, Samuel, was often absent from home due to his attempts to avoid confrontation with his wife, Rose. However, Maslow argued that situational factors alone rarely serve as *exclusive* explanations for behaviour, as the environment (situation) itself must be understood in terms of the character of the person within it. In Samuel's case, aside from his unhappy marriage, he 'loved whiskey and women and fighting'. Using this example, it is clear that his character supplemented any environmental explanations of his behaviour – one does not negate the other.

12. While considering individuals as integrated 'wholes', we must also consider the possibility that, due to limited capacities under certain circumstances, sometimes they are not. Maslow reported never experiencing love or affection from his mother, maintaining his view of her as 'bad' or ignorant.

Dealing with the breakdown of her marriage may have left Rose without the additional resources required to pacify the emotional demands of a young Maslow; frustrated, her response was to berate him, or worse. Generally, individuals are typically integrated (whole) when life is manageable. But, when life becomes too much, they disintegrate.

13. Motivation theory is not synonymous with behaviour theory. While behaviour is often motivated to gratify basic needs, this is not always the case because, as explained in the propositions above, it is almost always biologically, culturally and situationally determined as well. Self-actualization, as one exception, is better seen as an unmotivated growth or development from within – revelling in the joy of expressive behaviours such as art and music purely for the enjoyment of it, for example – as opposed to coping behaviours, which are motivated by the desire to get something done. While both behaviours can be determined, self-actualization is not motivated by need.

Hierarchy of Needs

Maslow centres his theory of motivation on what he calls the 'hierarchy of needs' (see Fig. 5). One key implication being that once a need has been satisfied, it no longer motivates behaviour. That is, *hungry* people may surrender their need for love in order to stay alive, but once their physiological needs (in this case food) have been met, they cease to exist as motivators. No longer

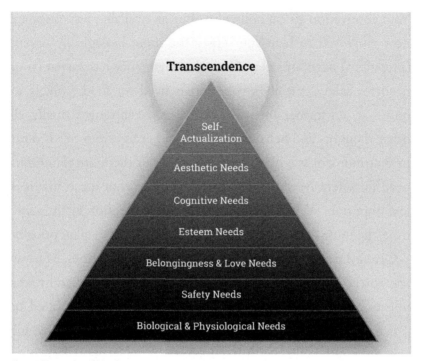

Fig. 5 Hierarchy of Needs

dominating the individual (unless thwarted), other higher needs, such as safety, emerge. Now, Maslow explains, the need for safety dominates the individual's thoughts and subsequent behaviour. When these new and higher needs are then satisfied, new (and higher still) needs, such as belongingness and love, emerge and so it continues. Being far from random though, this order of succession is organized into an evolving 'hierarchy of relative prepotency' whereby those needs with more biological urgency will be prioritized based upon their survival value.

Imagine skipping breakfast. You arrive at work so hungry that you cannot think of anything but food. Suddenly, the fire alarm goes off and the building is evacuated. In that situation, Maslow explains, it is unlikely that you are still thinking about food.

Your motivation to eat still exists, but all available responses are now employed to help you satisfy the more biologically urgent (prepotent) need for safety. Once the emergency has passed (your need for safety gratified), your earlier need for food is likely to return to its former intensity, once again eclipsing virtually all other thoughts and behaviours. But, just because your need to eat in that moment was abandoned in favour of the more clamorous need for safety, Maslow stresses that this does not mean that it is less important. When both needs demand attention at the same time, the more prepotent need – in this case, safety – takes priority.

Given the continual misinterpretations of his theories, Maslow was forced to clarify – more than once – that the hierarchy was not an automatic structuring whereby people are motivated to satisfy one need at a time. Instead, it is the result of a 'striving-to-overcome' generally (see Adler, Chapter 2) or, as Scott Kaufman (2020) puts it, 'two steps forward, one step back contiguous dynamic'. Likewise, at no point did Maslow explicitly state that everyone has the same needs activated in the same order or that any basic need requires absolute gratification before other, higher needs emerge – we can be *partially* satisfied in any of our needs, if not fully satiated. So, using the example above, had we eaten a snack to tide us over, the battle between hunger and safety needs would not have been as predatory. In a bid to explain at what percentage the average person might be satisfied at each level of the hierarchy, Maslow assigned arbitrary figures, or degrees, of relative satisfaction. For instance, 85 per cent in their physiological needs, 70 per cent in their safety needs, 50 per cent in their love needs, 40 per cent in their esteem needs and 10 per cent in their self-actualization needs. Thinking in these terms also helps explain how we can attend to multiple needs simultaneously. In Maslow's defence, Kaufman (2020) goes on to explain that 'the human condition isn't a competition, it's an experience' – the emergence of new needs is 'not like a video game where you reach one level [...] then some voice from above is like, "Congrats, you've unlocked esteem and then we never have to worry about that again"'. Instead, it is equilibrial: the gradual emergence of a new need (for example, esteem) occurs with partial satisfaction of the prepotent (more biologically urgent) need for food. Here, if hunger is only 10 percent satisfied, the need for esteem may not be apparent at all. However, as hunger reaches 75 percent gratification, the need for esteem may have emerged by 50 percent, and so on. As such, Maslow (1954) suggests that the hierarchy might be better understood in terms of 'decreasing percentages of satisfaction as we go up the hierarchy of prepotency'.

The eloquence of this formulation cannot be disputed but, given its complexity, this might explain the symbolic representation of the hierarchy as the pyramid illustrated in Fig. 5. First simplified for business managers by Douglas McGregor (1906–1964) – MIT Management professor and former pupil of Maslow – in his book *The Human Side of Enterprise* (1960), the first rendition of the hierarchy as a pyramid was introduced that same year in the journal *Business Horizons* in the paper 'How Money Motivates Men' by Charles McDermid, a consulting psychologist. But although both men failed to acknowledge the nuances that Maslow proposed for his hierarchy in their symbolic representation – which undoubtedly contributed to the misinterpretations and the perpetuation of the unfair criticisms received – Maslow showed little interest in taking on yet another battle. Not only was his health and financial situation crippling him at the time that the pyramid appeared, but he was feeling totally under-appreciated for his contributions to psychology. Dumbing down his theory any more than he thought he already had was clearly not an option for Maslow. That the management community seemed to be hanging on his every word (and their own interpretations of them by all accounts) on this occasion it is perhaps understandable that he was willing to let sleeping dogs lie. Retrospectively, this might not have been the wisest of moves.

Deficiency Needs (D-*needs*)

Basic, or deficiency needs (D-*needs*), include physiological needs, safety needs, social needs and esteem needs. Maslow sees these needs as arising due to deprivation and explains that the motivation to satisfy each one *decreases* as each need is met but increases the longer each need is denied. For example, the longer we go without food, the hungrier we become and the more motivated we are to find food. For Maslow (1943), deficiency needs can be identified as 'basic' or instinctoid if:

    i.   their absence produces illness

    ii. their presence prevents illness

    iii. satisfying the needs cures the illness

    iv. satisfying these needs takes priority over other satisfactions

    v.   they are inactive, or functionally absent, because the person is healthy

Maslow refined his theory throughout his lifetime based upon his own progressively sophisticated understanding of humans' potential. His original publication (1943, second edition 1954) includes the basic, or deficiency needs, as well as self-actualization – a 'being' or growth need (see Chapters 4 and 5). Although the conventional five-stage model is still considered to be Maslow's most seminal, and certainly the most enduring thanks to the likes of McGregor and McDermid, it is inaccurate when used as a description of his later thoughts. Expanded to include cognitive and aesthetic needs (1970a) and later transcendence needs (1970b), his final eight-stage model is the one that we will be focusing on throughout the remainder of this book.

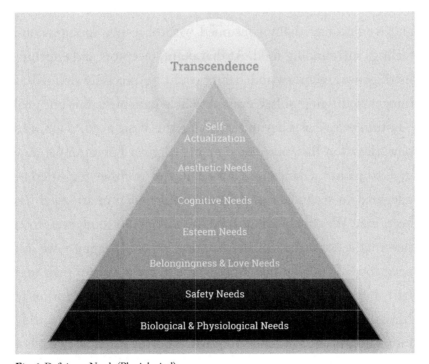

Fig. 6 Deficiency Needs (Physiological)

Physiological Needs

On any image related to motivation theory, regardless of how current, *physiological* needs – the basic requirements for human survival such as air, food, water, shelter and sex – are always considered as the starting point in terms of humans' motivation to act. As the human body cannot function at its best (maintain equilibrium or, in extreme cases, survive) without these physiological requirements, they take precedence over all other 'secondary' needs until gratified. In a situation where we feel both hungry and unloved, as explained above, we would be motivated to gratify our hunger most of all. This 'cognitive priority' is symbolized in the hierarchy in Fig. 6.

Maslow explains that if *none* of our physiological needs are being met, then all other needs are overshadowed or forgotten, and we become totally consumed with obsessive thoughts and feelings surrounding food. At that point, receptors and effectors, intelligence, memory and habits could be precisely defined as hunger gratifying tools, recruited to help us achieve this one goal – nothing else exists beyond satisfying this basic need. Capacities powerless for this purpose remain inactive. For example, any urge to paint or dance loses its value and is either forgotten or relegated to secondary importance until that primary need has been met. We dream about food, we talk about food, even food that might not ordinarily be tempting looks appealing – we just need food! It is now that Maslow's statement 'such a man may fairly be said to live by bread alone' stands true (1943). Curiously, Maslow noted that an individual's whole philosophy regarding future events changes once dominated by any palpable need. For example, in this deprived state, they may believe that if they had guaranteed access to, say, food for the rest of their life, they would want for nothing more. Promises of being 'good' from now on are generously made in exchange for the fulfilment of our needs and while this state of mind might seem inconceivable to the individual whose stomach is full, thoughts of other higher needs, such as love or respect, are useless as they cannot directly help the person satisfy their immediate need for food.

Still, while we cannot deny that hunger is a real issue that exists in some populations, in a normally functioning society extreme conditions are rare and we are able to tolerate periods of chronic deprivation, if necessary, to focus on more pressing needs. Even if hungry – we know that at some point soon, food will be available. In fact, Maslow argues, when the average American claims to be hungry, they are instead experiencing 'appetite' – a craving for something to eat regardless of whether they are hungry or not. In Chapter 4, we will discover that what Maslow was really interested in was what motivated people whose physiological needs had all been met: 'it is quite true that man lives by bread alone—when there is no bread', he says 'but what happens to man's desires when there is plenty of bread and when his belly is chronically filled?' (Maslow, 1943).

Safety Needs

Maslow proposed that once the physiological needs are relatively gratified, safety needs now motivate the individual's behaviour, albeit to a lesser degree. Like physiological needs, Maslow explains that safety needs (security; stability; freedom from fear, anxiety and chaos; law and order, and so on) now gather up all the individual's capabilities to achieve gratification. Receptors and effectors, intelligence, memory and habits that were previously employed to gratify hunger, are now utilized as safety-gratifying tools. The individual becomes consumed by obsessive thoughts surrounding safety – nothing exists beyond satisfying this need and almost all other needs become insignificant, including physiological needs which – now satisfied – cease to exist at this point in time.

Maslow (1943) argued that detecting safety needs in adults is difficult as they typically suppress fear reactions to avoid appearing weak or vulnerable. For example, we may not express our right to free speech for fear of repercussions if our views conflict with those of the majority – today's 'cancel culture' gives evidence of those acting as arbitrary judges of what is considered right or wrong and the subsequent punishments doled out to those who disagree. Children, on the other hand, are less skilled in this respect, making fear easier to observe.

You will remember from Chapter 1 that Harlow's research on rhesus monkeys left him refuting the behaviourist explanation that attachments are based upon the need for food. Extrapolating the monkey's behaviour to human infants, Maslow claimed that a child's tendency to cling to parents during moments of uncertainty, regardless of whether the parent is responsive to their needs or not, is testimony to the perceived role of the parent as the protector. This is quite distinct from the parent's role as provider of food or love and is evidence of the child's innate need for safety, regardless of how it presents itself. Maslow gives a touching insight into how his own parents' behaviour thwarted his need for safety, writing 'parental outbursts of rage or threats of punishment directed to the child, calling him names […] sometimes elicit such total panic and terror that we must assume more is involved than the physical pain alone' (Maslow, 1943). Failing to fulfil safety needs makes it unlikely that the higher needs for belongingness or love will emerge at that point in time, leaving the child socially isolated and alone and thus, hampering further progression towards reaching their potential.

Stressing the importance of a loving and predictable home, Maslow says that children who usually have their safety needs met tend only to show fear in extreme ways when in situations where adults might also feel unsafe. Ordinarily, if their safety needs are met then, just as a sated individual does not feel hungry, a safe individual feels no danger.

Belongingness and Love Needs

After both the physiological and safety needs have been relatively satisfied, the need for *love* and *belongingness* now motivates the individual and all available resources are ploughed into achieving this one goal. Perhaps contemplating his separation from Bertha during his early university days, or the friendships he lost along the way, Maslow (1943) writes:

> *'Now the person will feel keenly, as never before, the absence of friends, or a sweetheart, or a wife, or children. He will hunger for affectionate relations with people in general, namely, for a place in his group or family, and he will strive with great intensity to achieve this goal. He will want to attain such a place more than anything else in the world and may even forget that once, when he was hungry, he sneered at love as unreal or unnecessary or unimportant.'*

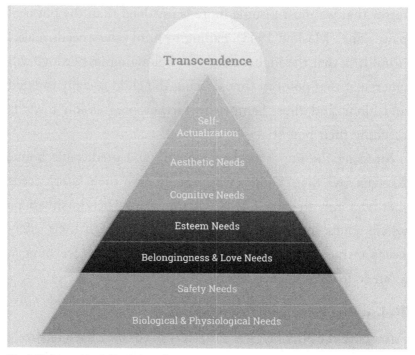

Fig. 7 Deficiency Needs (Psychological)

As the motivation to fulfill deficiency needs is a dynamic process active throughout life, Maslow warns that the deficiency motivated individual is more dependent on others than individuals motivated by growth towards self-actualization. Consequently, in terms of needing to belong, they are more invested in interpersonal relationships as a result of the purpose that others serve in terms of gratifying these needs as they arise; hence, they have more to fear if rejected.

Maslow offers few scientific particulars regarding the belongingness needs except that they are fundamental to our species. Having observed that these needs appeared to be increasing, Maslow (1954) blamed the scattering of families through increased mobility (with the advent of automobiles and the improvement of public transport), the collapse of traditional groupings and the continuous urbanization which had contributed towards the disappearance of the face-to-face interactions synonymous with village life. He argues that society has trivialized the importance of a neighbourhood; of being part of a gang or mixing with one's own kind; of man's deep desire to simply 'belong'.

But regardless of how much we understand a human's need for food, safety or the need to belong, Maslow believes we can never fully understand an individual's need for love. Making a clear distinction between two types of love, Maslow proposes that deficiency love, or D-love, is typically experienced during periods of extreme loneliness. Demonstrated in anxious, desperate, selfish, possessive displays of love in a bid to satisfy a deficiency, or need, within ourselves, other people are viewed only in terms of how they might be used; thus, distinct characteristics, not useful to the perceivers' needs, are overlooked or considered boring or irritating. We might picture deficiency motivated individuals demanding 'Feed me, keep me safe, love me, respect me'; and if we can't? 'Then get out of my way so that I can find someone who can'. Given that these needs can only be satisfied through the approval and affection of other people, deficiency motivated individuals are beholden to the whims and wishes of these others lest they jeopardize their source of fulfilment. Ergo, Maslow explains, a person in this dependent position can never truly be in control of his or her own destiny.

Being love (B-love), on the other hand, is less selfish and therefore, capable of greater love for others. Though highly unlikely, Maslow thought it would be the ideal situation to have two B-love individuals together. Based on a total acceptance of others just as they are, B-love involves genuine concern for what is best for them. Non-possessing and pleasure-giving, B-love is described by Maslow as having the same effect as aesthetic or mystic experiences – the highest level of human experience beyond the physical existence – that will be discussed shortly; we can never get enough and it requires no gratification. Through self-love, the individual is less fearful or neurotic; naturally, then, B-love is considered the healthier, more enjoyable and sustainable type of love, and the one most naturally displayed by self-actualizing people (see Chapter 4).

The thwarting of the need to be loved and to belong, Maslow reminds us, denies individuals the opportunity to both give and receive love, leaving them ill-equipped to cope with the demands of a normal social environment. Consequently, progression beyond the basic needs is unlikely.

Esteem Needs

Once all prepotent needs have been relatively satisfied, the need for *esteem* now becomes the most dominant motivator of an individual's behaviour. The highest category of all deficiency needs, Maslow (1943) classifies esteem needs into two subsidiary sets: esteem for oneself (or self-esteem), as demonstrated through feelings of confidence, adequacy, and freedom; and esteem in terms of status, reputation or respect from others. At its core, esteem refers to the need to simply feel genuinely good about oneself. At this level of the hierarchy nothing else matters beyond the desire to accomplish goals and contribute to the world around us. But, like Maslow himself, we also need our achievements and efforts to be recognized and appreciated in order to reinforce our value and self-worth and, thus, the confidence to move towards actualization. Maslow says that esteem for oneself typically requires less maintenance as it needs no external reinforcement or validation from others; rather, it is an individual's subjective evaluation of their own worth. If we have confidence in our own abilities to sing or dance, for example, negative feedback from others is unlikely to deter us. Through accomplishment, self-esteem becomes a permanent part of who we are, making it harder for others to take away. Sadly, being more self-critical, people low in self-esteem typically experience feelings of inferiority and helplessness which prevent them from moving up the hierarchy. Neglecting these needs can lead to either basic discouragement or else compensatory or neurotic trends – psychological defense mechanisms used to compensate for, or conceal, self-perceived inferiority – behaviours that ultimately stunt growth, as explained by Adler in Chapter 2.

Preconditions for Basic Need Satisfactions

While Maslow believes that basic needs – the physiological needs, the need for safety, belongingness and love, and self-esteem – are our way of coping with life, he also stresses that, in order for them to be satisfied, certain prerequisites must first be met. Cognitive needs such as freedom of speech, freedom to express and defend oneself, freedom of movement and justice, and honesty and equality, are all necessary preconditions, without which it would be highly improbable that the basic needs would be met. If society could create these preconditions, Maslow says, the best of humanity would evolve.

Although not included in the hierarchy, Maslow believes that failure to meet these preconditions would provoke the same emergency reaction in a person as failing to satisfy the basic need itself due to denying them the necessary or basic human 'rights', which would empower them in terms of taking control of their own fate.

Imagine movement up through the deficiency levels of the hierarchy as a game of Snakes and Ladders. The ladders are the necessary preconditions affording us the freedoms to gratify each need as it arises; each rung of the ladder, by design, facilitates movement towards self-actualization. But climbing the ladder is exhausting and requires total commitment and high self-esteem. Now imagine being faced with a snake at each rung of that ladder; these snakes represent the doubts as to whether you have what it takes to continue. You have two choices: continue despite any doubts or slide back down to the safe, familiar place of the lower levels. According to Maslow, those denied these basic human rights – these cognitive needs for freedom and equality – will often have little choice in these situations, making it unlikely that they will ever actualize their potential. Positive life experiences in terms of basic need gratification unquestionably help establish strong foundations for life. If encouraged, self-confidence and self-esteem lead to the utilization of successful coping mechanisms in adverse situations, ensuring that opting for the ladders will become a matter of course. Conversely, those whose needs are not met lack the self-esteem required to exercise self-governance and so look to others for validation and approval, more often than not resulting in less-than-optimal outcomes.

While Maslow warned that persistent denial of the deficiency needs will certainly lead to pathology, gratification of any of these needs – insofar as we can speak of each of them in isolation – is a move in a healthy direction towards actualization.

4. The Journey Towards Self-Actualization

'Let there be satisfaction of all the more prepotent motives—and then you will see that the higher human motives do come to the fore to take their turn on stage. It is not that they have only now come into existence. They have been there all the while, rooted deeply in the very core of human nature. It is only that they have heretofore been eclipsed by the more biologically urgent motives.' (Maslow, 1962)

As far back as 1943, in his paper 'A Theory of Human Motivation', Maslow recognized that his hierarchy of needs was incomplete. He mentions cognitive and aesthetic needs, but he does not include them within the fundamental motivational levels. It was at this point that Maslow's work went in two separate directions. The first was applying his theories to the workplace and the second was studying people who he considered to be self-actualizers. This chapter will first look at the difference between those individuals who choose safety over growth, and those who are motivated by cognitive

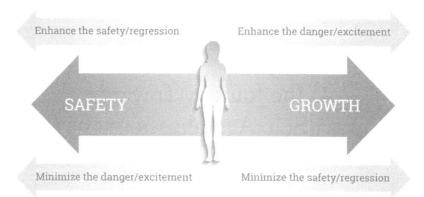

and aesthetic needs – precursors to self-actualization. It will then go on to explain the seventh level in Maslow's hierarchy, namely self-actualization, before finally touching upon the eighth and final level of self-transcendence and the plateau experience.

Given that our focus is now growth needs, it is important to recognize the shift in terminology used by Maslow when referring to this level of motivation. Now he speaks of growth motivation (in contrast to deficiency motivation), being or B-needs (in contrast to deficiency or D-needs), and of course, the ultimate goal – self-actualization. In contrast to deficiency needs, B-needs do not involve balance or homeostasis. Once satisfied, deficiency needs no longer motivate the individual to act. Growth needs, though, continue to be felt and may even become stronger once engaged. Once reasonably satisfied, the person moves closer to fulfilling their potential; closer to self-actualization.

Maslow believed that every human is born with the desire, and potential, to achieve self-actualization – to realize or fulfil their potentialities in becoming the ideal or best version of themselves. Not striving towards becoming someone or something they thought they were, or possibly wished they were, but becoming more and more who they, as an individual, were meant to be. Sadly, as will become familiar throughout the next two chapters, many see their progress disrupted through failure to meet their deficiency needs first.

Ungratified Deficiency Needs

Maslow's early assumption was that, once esteem needs had been sated, individuals would now be motivated towards self-actualization. But, while many of his students proved enthusiastic participants in his quest for the self-actualizing person, their responses to his chosen measures of emotional security and psychological adjustment forced him to question whether 20-year-olds were even capable of self-actualization or, as he was oft to put it, of being 'good human beings'. Although

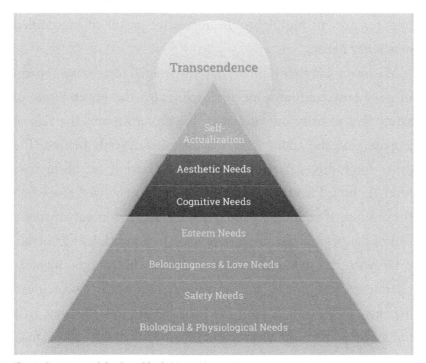

Fig. 8 Cognitive and Aesthetic Needs (Growth)

it was clear to him that they were well enough adjusted and appeared happy and untroubled, they had no apparent feelings of responsibility, were not goal oriented and showed little excitement when discussing future events. These observations troubled Maslow and his objectives began to diminish. Dejected, he felt confidence in just one of the students and his potential towards actualization but questioned whether the rest of them could even be considered 'nice'.

Over time, Maslow deduced that growth towards self-actualization only happens when the subjective experience of taking each step forward is more satisfying than the last. These steps are spontaneous and instinctive, he says, rather than purposeful or motivated by deficiency, and therefore lead to a greater understanding of the self. Still, the fact that not everyone opts for growth highlights the regressive power of ungratified deficiency needs.

Maslow holds that humans have existential forces that remain in persistent conflict. One force clings to the lower levels of safety and security out of fear of the unknown and the risk of jeopardizing the status quo (see Cognitive Needs below). The other force drives us towards self-actualization at the highest level. As both forces involve fear and excitement, we grow when the promise of excitement and the fear of regression outweigh the fear of danger and the preference for safety and lack of growth.

Growth is continuous throughout life and involves relentless decisions regarding whether to progress or regress. Self-actualization does not just happen, Maslow explains; it is not a matter of one great moment but, instead, the result of small accessions accumulated step by step over time. Ever the optimist,

Maslow believes that in a synergetic society (where the interests of both the individuals and the group are in harmony as a whole), if individuals are working under the best conditions with genuinely free choices, if they are not too young, too sick or too afraid to choose, then they will always opt for growth regardless of the commitment or danger involved.

However, ungratified safety needs are powerful and can override any courage the individual has mustered, preventing growth. Nobody but the individual knows when the time is right to step forward, says Maslow; it must be their choice based upon their assessment of each situation. Only the individual knows whether the promise of excitement outweighs the fear of regression. We cannot know it for them, Maslow says, and only when their fears or deficiency needs are respected will they feel brave enough to grow.

Maslow argued that actualization is always possible because humans are inherently good and so capable of making reasoned decisions regarding right and wrong or good and evil. His despondency towards theories that assume that the instinctoid aspects of human nature are limited to the physiological needs (see Chapter 3) led him to include the higher impulses for cognition and aesthetics into the later versions of his theory.

Cognitive Needs

At the beginning of the 20th century, little was known about cognitive impulses, their dynamics or pathology, largely – according to Maslow (1954) – because cognitive psychopathology 'does not cry for help'; subtle, it is easily overlooked or defined as normal. As such, cognitive impulses were not considered useful, at least in the clinical setting. But Maslow was convinced that knowledge (cognition) is imperative to satisfying the 'conative' needs – basic, universal needs that are motivational in nature such the physiological, safety, love and belongingness, esteem and self-actualization needs discussed so far. Needless to say, in order to satiate hunger, a person must *know* how to attain food. Necessarily then, cognitive needs, including 'curiosity' and 'the desire to know and to understand', were added to Maslow's original five-stage theory.

As with all other needs, Maslow postulates that the more we know, the more curious we become, and thus enter into a continuous search for meaning. The need to know and to understand are also instinctoid and apparent from early infancy as a spontaneous consequence of maturation, as opposed to being learned. We need only compare a child's level of curiosity to an adult's to appreciate that they do not need to be *taught* to be inquisitive. But Maslow was concerned that outside forces, such as impatient parents or uninspiring educators, can actually teach children *not* to be curious. Take for instance a time when you were learning about the weather as it was raining or snowing – were you taken outside to experience it directly, or was your attention continuously brought back to less exciting images of similar weather on the whiteboard at the front of the class? In *Toward a Psychology of Being*, Maslow warns that, in stifling curiosity, lying to people or denying them access to information, we put them in danger of becoming sceptical, cynical and disillusioned; in other words, pathological (psychologically unhealthy, ill). What we don't know has power over us, he explains, but knowing it brings it under our control and makes it subject to our choice; ignorance, he warns, makes real choice impossible.

In obstructing cognitive needs, Maslow (1954) warns, *all* conative needs are threatened because they are weak. As such, self-awareness in terms of knowing exactly what we want and need in terms of love, respect and knowledge for example, is extremely difficult to achieve. Not only this but the higher they are positioned on the hierarchy, the weaker and more easily manipulated or suppressed they become in response to environmental stressors, reducing the individual's chances of becoming self-actualized. They therefore need protecting.

Freud's psychoanalytic theory, written in 1901, states that psychological illness is the fear of knowing ourselves; fear of our potential or destiny (one of Freud's greatest discoveries, according to Maslow). In parallel with this, Maslow's theory states that any anxiety provoked by the fear of knowing diminishes our *desire* to know. So, if we are to fully understand the need to know, Maslow suggests integrating it with the more prepotent, or biologically urgent needs for 'safety' and 'security' as discussed in Chapter 3. In other words, the only way to reduce the perceived threat of the unfamiliar is to know and understand it. For example, children will be less afraid of not acing the end-of-year exam if they know that their parents will appreciate that they tried their best. Evading personal growth is a defensive act as it avoids exposure to the possibility of failure, judgement and inadequacy.

Aesthetic Needs

In contrast, aesthetic needs, including the need for symmetry, order and beauty in whatever form it is perceived, are neither basic nor universal in nature. From early cave dwellers to the present day, people have produced art for the pure enjoyment of it. At the time that Maslow was writing there was very little empirical literature on aesthetics. As was his habit, therefore, his research relied purely on his own intuition and clinical–personological studies of selected individuals, including Bertha and his daughter Ann, both talented artists in their own right. Aesthetic needs, he speculated, are so affecting and our hunger for beauty so desperate that Maslow admitted finding it difficult to resist the urge to advance his theories to correspond to these aesthetic experiences. Rejecting colleagues' suggestions that it would be difficult to measure such subjective experiences, Maslow offered suggestions as to how others could scientifically study responses to aesthetically beautiful experiences to demonstrate their validity, including measures of increased heart rate or horripilation (goosebumps).

However, Maslow made it perfectly clear that he was uninterested in conducting the research himself. His own observations gave him confidence enough to claim that, in the same way that people respond when their deficiency needs are not met, individuals with strong aesthetic needs react in much the same way – they become frustrated when these needs go unsatisfied, but actualized when they are fulfilled. As with the cognitive needs, satisfaction of aesthetic needs is consistent with psychological health; deprivation, says Maslow, leads only to pathology.

Self-actualization (Self-fulfillment Needs)

As discussed in Chapter 2, Maslow was not the first psychologist to put forward the concept of self-actualization. Originally conceived by Kurt Goldstein (1934), self-actualization was defined as the driving force that maximizes and determines the path of any organism whose innate goal is to actualize itself 'as it is'; viz, at any point in an organism's lifespan rather than a goal to be reached in the future. According to Maslow (1954) though, motivation towards self-actualization is an evolutionary development unique to humans: 'We share the need for food with all living things, the need for love with (perhaps) the higher apes, the need for self-actualization with nobody. The higher the need, the more specifically human it is,' he explained. Through self-actualizers, Maslow was confident that humankind would have a model, or 'prototype', of the fully growing and self-fulfilling human being and, thus, the ultimate values by which we should live (see Chapter 5).

While Maslow attributes self-actualization to Goldstein in 'A Theory of Human Motivation', he angered Goldstein by openly disagreeing with his suggestion that self-actualization *determines* one's life. Instead, he argued that it *motivates* the individual to realize their potential – their biological destiny – bringing them closer to the realm of Being. Whereas ungratified deficiency needs can be harmful or unpleasant, self-actualization works differently because, while it can make a person happier, life can still be fulfilling if neglected. Thus, in contrast to Goldstein's driving force, Maslow explains self-actualization as a more gradual process of personal growth, or development, that only becomes possible once people feel safe, loved and respected. Only then will they possess enough confidence to 'become what thou ought' (Nietzsche quoted in Maslow, 1943).

Individuals satisfying all prior needs and reaching self-actualization are fundamentally called 'satisfied' people and it is from these people that Maslow believed we would see the greatest levels of happiness, contentment and fulfillment. That said, Geller (1982) draws our attention to the 'anomie, alienation, boredom, apathy, resignation, cynicism, joylessness, meaningless, and despair' experienced by some in the West, despite having all their basic needs met. It is in response to such observations that Maslow explains that, although individuals *should* now be striving towards self-actualization, they would always experience a new discontent and restlessness unless they are doing what they are most suited for as an individual. Accordingly, 'a musician must make music, an artist must paint, a poet must write, if he is to be ultimately at peace with himself' (Maslow, 1954). It stands to reason, then, that gratification of self-actualization needs will differ from person to person. Unfortunately, reaching this level of growth rarely happens – less than 2% of the adult population in Maslow's opinion based upon his own preliminary research – making satisfied people the exception, not the rule.

Characteristics of Self-actualizers

Upon meeting Benedict and Wertheimer (see Chapter 2), Maslow grew increasingly excited and more confident about his emerging theory of human motivation. Although the theory had received little exposure, Maslow was certain that it would gain the kudos it deserved in time. It wasn't until 1945 though that he began more formally documenting his evolving notion of self-actualization in what he called a 'good human being notebook'. With no prior research to guide him, Maslow used the terms 'good human being' and 'self-actualization' interchangeably at first, perhaps highlighting an acknowledgement that he was ill prepared for what was potentially an overwhelming challenge.

Having long since abandoned the idea of utilizing his students in his research, even the older participants he identified as potentially self-actualizing eventually disappointed Maslow. They either failed to live up to his expectations of what a good human being looked like, or they refused to take part altogether. Although he would later comment that this reluctance may have been a general disinclination towards sharing themselves with the world, preferring instead to remain detached and maintain their privacy − a characteristic of self-actualization (see point 5 below) − at the time, he was puzzled. With his intellectual pride at stake, Maslow had little choice but to accept that emotional security and psychological adjustment were not dependable predictors of a good, or self-actualized, human being; 'The cow, the slave, the robot may all be well adjusted,' Maslow (1954) says, highlighting that these predictors set a very low ceiling when considering humans' potential for growth. Changing tack, rather than questioning 'what makes a genius like Beethoven?' Maslow began questioning the difference between those who are, or desire to be, growth motivated or self-actualized and those who live only to gratify basic needs. 'Why aren't we all Beethovens?' he wondered. With his renewed focus and a necessary change in the criteria of self-actualization, he began making progress.

Over time, Maslow noticed that his observations of Benedict and Wertheimer were becoming less those of individuals in their own right, and more like composites of the self-actualizing person. He realized that he was describing a *type* of person, rather than two incomparable individuals. Before long, characteristics of the self-actualizing person were revealed in one person after another. Besides them all being older and visibly successful,

Maslow appeared confident that, in observing these people, he would gain invaluable insight into what all humans are capable of achieving. After almost six years of keeping his theory under wraps, Maslow wrote an article entitled 'Self-actualizing People: A Study of Psychological Health' (1950) identifying 14 common features of the self-actualizing person, which he later expanded upon in *Motivation and Personality*.

Common Features of the Self-actualizing Person

1. They perceive reality efficiently and can tolerate uncertainty

2. They accept themselves and others for who they are

3. They are spontaneous in thought and action

4. They are problem-centred (not self- or ego-centred)

5. They are often detached and have a need for privacy

6. They are capable of deep appreciation of basic life-experience

7. They are open to peak experiences

8. They are concerned for the welfare of humanity, referred to as *Gemeinschaftsgefühl*

9. They prefer a few meaningful relationships over many superficial ones

10. They are democratic, respectful and open to ideas

11. They have a strong moral code of ethical conduct

12. They are philosophical with a good-natured sense of humour

13. They are creative and inventive

14. They are resistant to enculturation and reject ineffectual cultural norms

Describing the self-actualizer 'not as an ordinary man with something added, but rather as the ordinary man with nothing taken away', Maslow (1946) made it clear that all humans have the potential to achieve actualization given the right circumstances to grow. Maslow's assertion – that the motivational life of self-actualizing people is both quantitatively and qualitatively different from that of ordinary people – was acclaimed for its philosophical boldness. But, concerned that novelists, poets and essayists had begun exaggerating the characteristics of the good humans as being almost too good so that nobody would like to be like them, Maslow (1954) insists that self-actualizers are far from perfect. However, using them as biological assays for studying humans' optimum potentiality, he urged, should not be overlooked. So convinced was he that, during a radio talk show for the Pacifica Foundation at Berkeley in 1960, he introduced his vision of Eupsychia – a psychologically healthy utopia inhabited by 1,000 self-actualizers and their families – and asked the audience to consider the following: What educational system would they establish? What religion would they follow? What level of governance would they develop? In doing so, he was inviting his audience to seriously consider what sort of a society would evolve if all members were willing to forsake material wealth for one in which everyone's needs, both deficiency and growth needs, were nurtured in an environment that was conducive to each member reaching their full potential.

Critique

Given the limitations of Maslow's methodology and the lack of any verifiable data, his certainty regarding self-actualization has been questioned. Relying on biographical analysis – an interpretive research approach to understand individuals and make sense of their behaviours in social contexts – Maslow analyzed incomplete data from just 18 people who met his a priori criterion for the self-actualizer. Some of these he knew, while others – including Albert Einstein and Eleanor Roosevelt – he was unlikely to have known well enough to make a definitive judgement one way or the other beyond their collective concerns with issues of great relevance to humanity. The unusually small sample size, together with accusations of the meaning or value of Maslow's work being determined by his intentional use of people he *expected* to meet his criterion for psychological health, left him vulnerable to further criticism regarding the kinds of generalizations that he often made about his theories on self-actualization.

Consequently, it is important to reiterate that the defining characteristics outlined by Maslow – aside from being inconsistent and ambiguous – are subjective and mere impressions gleaned from his singular interpretation of the data. Still, Maslow remained nonchalant. Having never tried to hide the fact that he had selected the 'equivalent of Olympic gold medal winners', he remained ahead of the blame game. In 'Self Actualization and

Beyond' (1965) he writes, 'My generalizations grew out of MY selection of certain kinds of people [...] obviously, other judges are needed,' rendering familiar criticisms stale.

Over the years, Maslow was repeatedly forced to reiterate his position that, contrary to the common misinterpretation presumably generated by those who insist on referencing only his original five-stage model in their work, self-actualization is not the perfect end state. Having only observed the characteristics of self-actualizers in adults, he deduces that this stage of the hierarchy is only reached through the maturity that comes with age and life experience, although he never actually states that self-actualization is *exclusive* to those in their twilight years. Nevertheless, it is typically assumed that this level of achievement is the ultimate end goal, rather than being part of an active process; that it gives the impression of Being rather than 'becoming'. Suggesting that we regard growth as the process of bringing people *towards* self-actualization, Maslow thinks it might be easier to accept it as an *ongoing* process that occurs throughout life or to think of people as 'beings in the *process* of becoming'. Optimistically, he hoped that thinking in this way would also prevent the tendency to view each step towards self-actualization as the all-or-none affair that his critics alleged, arguing instead that 'basic needs and self-actualization do not contradict each other any more than childhood or maturity. One passes into the other and is a necessary prerequisite for it' (Maslow, 1968a). Despite his early trepidation, Maslow's theory of self-actualization was considered a conceptual breakthrough.

The Next Step

Austrian neurologist and psychiatrist Viktor Frankl (1905–1997) believed that the true meaning of life cannot be found within, but in a purpose greater than our own. Losing not only his pregnant wife, Tilly, but both parents and his only brother during the Holocaust, Frankl remained steadfast in his belief that unimaginable suffering had a purpose. In *Man's Search for Meaning* (1946), he outlines his belief that it is self-transcendence, not self-actualization, that best explains the main aim of humans' existence. Those who strive towards self-actualization as an end goal in itself, Frankl states, are missing the point that self-actualization is but a consequence of self-transcendence for it is only via committing to altruistic goals *outside* of the personal self – committing to the fulfillment of life's meaning – that actualization is attainable.

Given that no-one had their basic needs met in the concentration camps, Frankl's explanation that those who saw their existence as purposeful and meaningful were the ones most likely to survive, gave Maslow something to think about. He had already been expressing doubts about self-actualization as it currently stood and, regardless of how vehemently he defended his methods, he was completely aware of how open to criticism self-actualization was considering its focus entirely on the individual, excluding any concern for others. Yet, on noticing that many of his self-actualizers had simultaneously demonstrated actualization of their own potential but also appeared so selfless, Maslow's optimism grew. In his haste to write his great masterpiece, he was concerned that he had muddled the characteristics of self-actualized people with those of self-transcendent people. Later, we shall see that more clarity was provided when *peak experiences* were specifically used to define transcendence but, at this point in time, Maslow could no longer ignore the anxiety he had been feeling regarding the incompleteness of the hierarchy. It became abundantly clear to him that self-actualization was not the pinnacle of his pyramid – transcendence was – and Maslow knew that he was running out of the time he would need to dig deeper into his research on the human psyche.

Over the years, Maslow became increasingly convinced that self-actualization is merely the bridge to self-transcendence – a 'transitional goal, a rite of passage, a step along the path to transcendence of identity'. In *Religions, Values and Peak Experiences* (1964) he writes:

> *'The empirical fact is that self-actualizing people, our best experiencers, are also our most compassionate, our great improvers and reformers of society, our most effective fighters against injustice, inequality, slavery, cruelty, exploitation [...] it also becomes clearer and clearer that our best "helpers" are the most fully human persons. What I may call the bodhisattvic path is an integration of self-improvement and social zeal, i.e., the best way to become a better "helper" is to become a better person. But one necessary aspect of becoming a better person is via helping other people. So, one must and can do both simultaneously.'*

By 1966, in an essay called 'Critique of Self-Actualization Theory', Maslow was fully committed to Frankl's proposal, agreeing that self-actualization was not enough. He would go on to add the concept of transcendence as the final component of the complete model.

5. From Actualization to Transcendence

U niversally acknowledged for its optimistic and compelling ideas, *Motivation and Personality* energized Maslow and he was ready to focus his attention on the realm of ecstatic and mystical or transcendental experiences; a characteristic of self-actualizers he had observed over a decade before. Having amassed an extensive amount of material on the subject of mysticism – more so perhaps than any other American psychologist at that point in time – it is astonishing to learn that Maslow's papers were initially poorly received. A declared atheist, he too had been baffled at self-actualizers' reports of mystical-like experiences and so understood any initial reluctance, putting it down to the unorthodox nature of the topic. Given that behaviourism remained the mainstream psychology of the day at this point in time, he was not surprised that the concept of transcendence might appear too left field. But, as the papers were rejected by one major league journal after another, including *Psychological Review* and *American Psychologist*, he grew resentful. Not one to be beaten, Maslow used his position as president and keynote speaker of the American Psychological Society's Division of Personality and

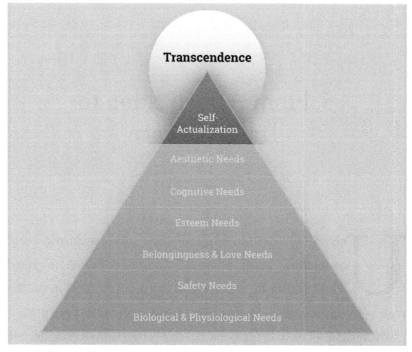

Fig. 9 Self-actualization

Social Psychology to present his paper 'Cognition of Being in the Peak Experience' on 1 September 1956, to a warmer reception. Although it would take another three years to publish due to its radical nature, with the political repression instigated by US Senator McCarthy finally coming to an end, there came about a longing for constructive change.

Transcendence

At the very peak of Maslow's hierarchy is his notion of transcendence:

> *[...] the very highest and most inclusive or holistic levels of human consciousness, behaving and relating, as ends rather than means, to oneself, to significant others,*

> *to human beings in general, to other species, to nature,*
> *and to the cosmos.'* (Maslow, 1971)

In his first attempt to provide some form of continuity between the 'ideal' and the 'average' person, Maslow admitted that it was almost impossible for him to be theoretically neat in his description of people who reach this level of growth. At times, this made it difficult for the layman to follow, particularly when he refers to self-actualizers as those motivated towards self-fulfilment in one instance, and in another, as people metamotivated by the B-values (see below). On finding 'not only self-actualizing persons who transcend, but also nonhealthy people, non-self-actualizers who have important transcendent experiences,' Maslow (1971) concludes that anyone can enjoy transcendent, or 'peak', experiences, regardless of whether or not they have reached self-actualization. It is during these experiences, he says, that an individual takes on the characteristics of self-actualizers in the way that they are 'more truly [themselves], more perfectly actualizing [their] potentialities, closer to the core of [their] Being, more fully human' – albeit fleetingly and temporarily (1962). In a nutshell, this is what Maslow meant in *Toward a Psychology of Being* when he described self-actualization as 'a matter of degree and of frequency rather than an all-or-none affair'. It is a kind of 'episode, or a spurt in which the powers of the person come together' in the most remarkable way. It goes without saying, he says, that if any of us go without food for long enough, eventually we will need to satisfy recurring feelings of hunger, regardless of how actualized we are, because deficiency motivations must be maintained and revisited as a matter of course. However, it is during those moments when deficiency motivations lie satiated that we are offered a glimpse of reality 'in its own Being [...] rather than as something to be used, or something to be afraid of, or to be reacted to in some other [deficiency-motivated] human way'.

Paradoxically, given Maslow's assertion that not all self-actualizers transcend, he argues that a person cannot claim to be fully actualized, or 'whole', until they have transcended. While characteristics of the self-actualizer include qualities like the selflessness seen in those who transcend, the goal of reaching self-actualization itself is the fulfillment of our *own* purpose or potential. Self-transcendence, on the other hand, is entirely altruistic, self-denying and ego-transcending in that the focus is on higher goals *outside* of the personal self. Individuals are at their healthiest, happiest and most fulfilled. They are at their most idiosyncratic, he explains, when putting personal needs aside to serve something greater than themselves, and it is during these precise moments in time that they feel detached from the mundane, trivial nature of their own everyday lives. Sensing that they are at one with the whole universe – really belonging to it rather than feeling like an outsider looking in – it is now that Maslow believes self-transcenders are experiencing what he calls the peak experience.

Peak Experiences

In 1962, Maslow consulted various sources: reports from self-actualizing people he knew, unsolicited letters from people interested in his new research, the phenomenological reports of colleagues, and 190 of his students who responded to the following prompt:

'I would like you to think of the most wonderful experience or experiences in your life; happiest moments, ecstatic moments, moments of rapture, perhaps from being in love, or from listening to music or suddenly "being hit" by a book or a painting, or from some great creative moment. First list these. And then try to tell me how you feel in such acute moments, how you feel differently from the way you feel at other times, how you are at that moment a different person in some ways.'
(Maslow, 1962)

From this, Maslow defined peak experiences as 'rare, exciting, oceanic, deeply moving, exhilarating, elevating experiences that generate an advanced form of perceiving reality, and are even mystic and magical in their effect upon the experimenter' (Maslow, 1964). In short, any experience that comes close to perfection. Asking people to report on their happiest, most ecstatic and rapturous moments was hardly going to reap a picture of doom and gloom but, having begun his research under the assumption that mystical experiences only happened to 'one saint every century,' Maslow questioned whether the experiences reported were signs of pathological illness.

Freud, who claimed never to have had such an experience, described the 'oceanic feeling' decades before as nothing more than 'a fragmentary vestige of a kind of consciousness possessed by an infant who has not yet differentiated himself or herself from other people and things' (Freud, 1961) – in other words, an incomplete awareness of the world that typically precedes the concept of the 'self' as independent from others and an acknowledgement that other people exist. This initially gave some weight to Maslow's concern that such reports were merely indications of psychopathy in adults and, combined with his mother's penchant for all things holy, gives some insight into why Maslow might associate any theistic reference to mental illness. But, coupled with the knowledge that those taking part in his phenomenological study were psychologically healthy, he knew that mental illness wasn't the answer. Never shy about admitting that –for him – God did not exist, Maslow was certain that such mystical experiences were not necessarily theistic; after all, he argues, wasn't Buddhism – which was more of a philosophy – a case in point?

This idea that people can have religious experiences without believing in God can be traced back to Feuerbach's *The Essence of Christianity* (1841) in which he wrote 'God was merely the projected essence of man' and as such 'Man [...] must be proclaimed first and recognized as the first [...] Man's God is man' (Feuerbach quoted in Vitz, 1994). An avid reader of Feuerbach, Maslow agreed that otherworldly experiences are possible regardless of any belief in a divine order and, however ecstatic, such experiences could be explained entirely within the concept of human nature and its hidden potential. As such, they could be enjoyed by anyone at any time, including children, regardless of how well they were able to articulate such moments. He writes:

> *'I myself once had the mystic experience [in which]*
> *I experienced a blind groping for something, an*
> *overwhelming sense of unsatisfied desire, a helplessness*

which was so intense that it left me weeping. [...] At
the moment of the mystic experience, we see wonderful
possibilities and inscrutable depths in mankind [...]
Why not ascribe [the wonder of the experience] to
man himself? Instead of deducing [...] the essential
helplessness and smallness of man [...] can we not
round out a larger, more wonderful conception of the
greatness of the human species [...]?' (Maslow quoted
in Kaufman, 2020)

His excitement growing, Maslow was intent on generalizing
this experience and revoking it from its traditionally religious or
supernatural association. That his ideas were met with scepticism
from his peers had long since become par for the course, but
Maslow remained undeterred. Peak experiences, Maslow
discovered, can be anything from simple activities such as a walk
in nature or watching a storm brew over a neighbour's rooftop,
to more intense events such as a first kiss or childbirth, because
'the sacred is in the ordinary' (Maslow, 1964). Yet, the perception
of such familiar experiences becomes richer than they were
before, almost unbearable in their intensity, and any concept of
time and space are now lost. Regardless of the catalyst though,
Maslow stresses that it is the complete absorption in, and the
subsequent emotion or validation felt *during* a peak that is key
to the profound and transformative effects left in its wake. In
Toward a Psychology of Being, it is hard to ignore any reference
to Maslow's 'near-death experience' back in 1946 when he says:
'Heaven, so to speak, lies waiting for us [...] to step into for a
time and to enjoy [...] we have been in it, we can remember it

forever, and feed ourselves on this memory and be sustained in times of stress [...] just one single glimpse of heaven,' he adds, 'is proof of its existence even if never experienced again'. In other words, regardless of how ungratifying, mundane or painful life may be, one common effect of peak experiences is that the person experiencing it is more likely to appreciate life as meaningful and, thus, worth living.

Such moments of awakening were unveiled by Wertheimer 25 years before in *Some Problems in the Theory of Ethics* where he claims that, during such moments we are reminded of our finest qualities as if they had been lost or forgotten along the way. Maslow agrees, reiterating that during a peak-experience, the person experiencing it is less likely to see the one true God, and more likely to see the best part of themselves. However, though intrinsically valuable, the peak experience itself has no further purpose; it is not a means to any external end, but rather the end itself and therefore is important in its own right. Contrary to the axiom that all behaviour is motivated, Maslow asks us to consider just 'Being'.

The Ineffability of the Peak Experience

In 1962, a chance friendship with Michael Murphy, co-founder of Esalen – an intentional community in Big Sur California fascinated by the influence of humanistic psychology – opened Maslow's eyes to the experiential methods used to enhance growth towards self-actualization and, thus, peak experiences. Around that time, Ellen Maslow was working as a research assistant to her father's friend, notorious psychologist Timothy Leary (1920–1996). Having shown initial interest in Leary's highly controversial work which involved the effects of psychedelic drugs on the mind, Maslow contemplated whether psilocybin – a hallucinogenic substance found in fungi and more commonly known as 'magic mushrooms' – could induce a peak-experience, as those at Esalen had claimed. Reminding ourselves of Maslow's assertion that a person could not claim to be fully actualized or 'whole' until they have transcended, it is understandable perhaps that pioneers like Leary may have wanted to open up this potential to the masses rather than it being limited to Maslow's 'few'. But, although Maslow conceded that these methods could work on the right people under the right circumstances, he remained steadfast in his belief that seeking transient states through hallucinogenic substances could not be seen as contributing towards the overall actualization of a person as, according to him, self-actualization is a lifelong process that requires work. Despite his best efforts to distance himself from Leary, who he viewed as appropriating his theories on humanism and rewriting them to suit his own purposes, Maslow became the reluctant hero for those seeking self-actualization. Preferring to be known for his intellectual prowess, however, he later publicly criticized Esalen's 'big bang' approach to personal transformation. Having once been extremely flattering of Esalen as a world-class educational institute, in 'Self-Actualization and Beyond', he found it difficult to hide his contempt for the 'multitudes of starry-eyed dilettantes – big talkers, great planners, tremendously enthusiastic – who come to nothing as soon as a little hard work is required,' and urged Murphy to promote hard work and discipline as essential to inner growth, rather than current pursuits of instant gratification via psychedelic drugs and weekend workshops.

Psychedelic drugs aside, Maslow believed that it is not possible to command a peak-experience whenever it takes your fancy. In *Religions, Values and Peak Experiences*, he explains that peaks happen without warning and, as such, are not to be counted upon; to go looking for them is like searching for happiness, a fruitless endeavour that is best not done directly. Unlike self-actualization, which is achievable for few, Maslow is convinced that most people have peak experiences at some point during their life. In fact, he says, anyone failing to report them is either renouncing them, denying them, is afraid of them or is forgetting them. While longing for a scientific way to talk about this phenomenon, Maslow realized that in the absence of any well-defined, common terminology specific to peak-experiences, they are beyond description for many. It is therefore only 'vivid peakers' who intuitively understand what they are experiencing. As a result, Maslow adopted what he called 'rhapsodic communications' – the figurative, poetic, metaphorical language often used to describe a dream or fantasy – in order to successfully focus 'weak-peakers'' attention inwards in a bid to reignite memories of experiences long since forgotten. 'I couldn't teach [a weak-peaker] how to have a peak-experience; but I could teach that he had already had it,' he declared confidently (Maslow, 1962).

Acute Identity in the Peak Experience

If we accept Maslow's theory that our end goal is self-transcendence, not self-actualizaton, we must also embrace his notion that the path to this state involves developing a strong sense of self – an identity – achieved through basic-need gratification. But, given Maslow's stance that motivation beyond the deficiency level is rare, he coined the terms 'metaneeds' and 'metamotivation', to indicate that certain needs, or motivations, are beyond what might be seen as characteristic of the whole human species. Where *all* people are motivated by the basic physiological, safety, belongingness and love, and esteem needs, once sated, he explained, only *healthy* (self-actualized) individuals are 'metamotivated' by what he called 'metaneeds' or B-values: intrinsic values of 'being' (see below) that only come into play once all deficiency needs have been met. These B-values, Maslow says, are the ideal goals of all human beings and, as such, they themselves are the metamotivations. Only those living amongst the B-values reach self-actualization, according to Maslow, and only they are capable of metamotivation. Those choosing to live outside of the B-values will sense a lack of meaning to their lives and will not reach actualization, regardless of whether they have satisfied their deficit needs or not. Taking this thought process further, he says:

> '*To average the choices of good and bad choosers, of healthy and sick people, is useless [...] I suspect that what is good for the healthy persons (chosen by them) may very probably be good for the less healthy people, too, in the long run, and is what the sick ones would also choose if they could become better choosers [...] I propose that we explore the consequences of observing whatever our best specimens choose, and then assuming that these are the highest values for all mankind.*' (Maslow, 1962)

Like his investigations into self-actualization, not only does Maslow use his own personal reports and readings of available literature to create an impressionistic, ideal, composite image of the peak experience, he paints an idealistic portrait of self-actualizers, or peakers, too, and through them the ultimate values by which we should live:

> **truth; goodness; beauty; wholeness; dichotomy-transcendence** (transcendence of dichotomies, contradictions); **aliveness; uniqueness; perfection; necessity** (inevitability); **completion; justice; order; simplicity; richness; effortlessness; playfulness** and **self-sufficiency**.

These particular characteristics of being, of the peak identity, are intrinsic to all of us, and, according to Maslow, essential to the concept of being fully human.

During the radio broadcast for the Pacifica Foundation at Berkeley (where Maslow first introduced his vision of Eupsychia), he was asked: How different is your approach to those of the philosophers or theologians, in terms of determining which values we should live by? Naturally, he claimed that by observing the best of mankind under the best conditions that he would be able to scientifically describe what those values are. Given that we are talking about values such as truth and justice, it seems improbable that anyone would take offence at Maslow's suggestions; but whether we like these values or not, questions are raised as to whether scientific psychology (observation methods in particular) can decide which values we live by. Accused of rooting his definition of psychological health on his own implicit values, Maslow remained unperturbed. In *Religions, Values and Peak Experiences*, he says:

'We can no longer rely on tradition, on consensus, on cultural habit, on unanimity of belief to give us our values. These agreed-upon traditions are all gone. Of course, we never should have rested on tradition as its failures must have proven to everyone by now it never was a firm foundation. It was destroyed too easily by truth, by honesty, by the facts, by science, by simple, pragmatic, historical failure.' (1962)

The following year, 1965, at a conference for the training of counsellors, Maslow continued to stress the importance of values in relation to psychological health: 'In certain definable and empirical ways,' he says, 'it is necessary for man to live in beauty rather than ugliness, as it is necessary for him to have food for an aching belly or rest for a weary body' (Maslow, 1965a). When denied **truth** for example, it is expected that people would develop paranoia; without **justice** and **order**, they would feel unsafe and, without **playfulness**, they would lose their zest for life. Consequently, denial of these metaneeds will lead to the metapathologies – the 'anomie, alienation, boredom, apathy, resignation, cynicism, joylessness, meaningless, and despair' – mentioned by Geller (1982) in Chapter 4. Thus, Maslow argues, both deficiency needs and metaneeds are biologically desirable due to their ability to foster biological success.

Maslow quickly noted that people's reported experiences of self-transcendence were so similar that they all appeared to come from the same person. If this observation were found to be true, he knew that it would fly in the face of the assumption in science that facts and values are mutually exclusive and, thus, cannot occur at the same time. Unable to resist one last dig at the experimentalists, Maslow once again spells out his stance – that values are intrinsic and as such must be acknowledged and understood. Facts, he reiterated, are steeped in values. But, given that his days of empirical research had finished decades before, the experimentalists fought back and questioned his right to offer relevant criticism. Rejecting his misguided accusations that rigorous experimentation prohibits subjective emotions such as awe and wonder, B.F. Skinner was famously quoted as saying 'I have had many peak experiences and they have not decreased as I have become more rational [...] You ought to get to know a behaviourist better!' (Hoffman, 1999). Many may have felt the intended sting of this remark, but Maslow revelled in the banter, regardless of how critical it was.

Plateau Experience

The realization that peak experiences cannot and do not last led Maslow to define the 'plateau experience': a term he co-opts from his colleague, Indian scientist and yoga practitioner U.A. Asrani. Largely influenced by the Eastern philosophy of Taoism, the plateau experience differs from the peak experience in that it is a gentle, sustained, serene cognitive state as opposed to an emotionally intense, climactic explosion which subsequently ends. Perhaps thinking about his own fragile state, Maslow stresses that because the ageing body is weak it would struggle to cope with the 'little death' and then rebirth of acute peak experiences. Though he describes this form of happiness (the peak experience) as obtainable and real, he reminds us that it is intrinsically transient and offers a mere glimpse of transcendence. Instead, situations experienced as if for the first time are replaced with the continuing joy and happiness associated with the less intense plateau experience. In fact, contrary to being unexpectedly hit by a peak experience, the plateau state of unitive consciousness *can* be cultivated through maturation, learning, discipline and commitment; that is to say, that it can be meaningfully aspired to over the course of one's lifetime.

Sadly, Maslow never got to explain how his conceptualization of the plateau process might unfold. Due to his rapidly failing health, he was unable to promote this additional level of his hierarchy with the same gusto as the others, and beyond making an appearance in anomalous publications, the plateau experience never enjoyed the same time and attention as all other needs. Instead, despite Maslow's insistence that 'The so-called spiritual [...] life is clearly rooted in the biological nature of the species' (Maslow, 1971), it remains largely unexplored by scientists seemingly relieved not to have to dabble in its religious connotations.

Conclusion

The importance of Maslow's theory of human motivation to the field of psychology and beyond is indisputable. His extraordinary prescience in terms of understanding what people need in order to achieve their potential, and how those needs differ between one person and another, resonated with many influential thinkers of his day. Almost 80 years after it was written, the theory of human motivation maintains its position as the most-often cited, the most popular and the most enduring motivational theory, even in today's globalizing world – largely due to its applicability to everyday life.

The hierarchy of needs represents an important shift in psychology and Maslow can be directly credited as one of the founders and driving forces behind the humanistic movement. With a focus on the uniqueness of each individual, Maslow fought hard for the intellectual community to appreciate that as a species, we are to be celebrated. Offering a new image of humans that showcases their courage and optimism, truth and compassion – an image totally at odds with the hopeless, dark pessimistic version offered by Freud or the one incapable of sentience that appeared the best the behaviourists could come up with – Maslow encouraged an awareness of what it means to be inherently good.

Nevertheless, one of the most prevailing criticisms of Maslow's work is its lack of scientific credibility. But, like Wertheimer before him, Maslow was more interested in writing theory than conducting experiments and contended that it was science's, not his, responsibility to find solutions to existential questions, using his suggested ideas as the framework. Hitting back, he said:

> *'I consider it quite scientific to work with vague concepts, doing the best we can in the face of complex problems [...] the true scientist lives in the land of possibility, the land of questioning rather than the area of final and complete answers. He is not content to rest on the achievements of his predecessors [...] the true scientist continually tries to extend the areas of knowledge and therefore [...] works primarily with questions rather than with answers.'*
> (Maslow quoted in Hoffman, 1999)

Accused of showing bias towards white, Western males, despite including women (Harriet Tubman) and people of colour (George Washington Carver) in his list of self-actualizers, the values and ideologies visible in his hierarchy have been criticized as being relevant only to individualistic cultures (whereby a society emphasizes the individual over the entire group – examples include the Anglosphere, as well as the Netherlands and Germany). Although both individualistic and collective cultures display the need to belong, collectivist cultures place little value on self-esteem, instead striving towards achieving societal goals. Tay and Diener (2011), for example, found that an individual can achieve self-actualization without fulfilling the more prepotent need to belong. However, their findings from across 124 studies did show universal support for Maslow's claim that, in satisfying one's most basic needs *first*, self-actualization is *more* likely.

Openly admitting that he did tend to pay more attention to people who showed more promise at the exclusion of those he deemed 'losers' or 'incapables', it is not surprising that Maslow was accused of being elitist. Still, at his core he was egalitarian. His whole career was focused on promoting equality for all and he genuinely believed that anyone not achieving their full potential in life could legitimately point the finger at social malfeasance and a general lack of *Gemeinschaftsgefühl* (community feeling or social interest). In *The Forgiving Life* (2012), Robert Enright suggests that, while some people's lot in life is harder to bear, our internal reactions to environmental changes can make all the difference in terms of human growth. With reference to the esteem marker in particular, he states that the virtues of humility and forgiveness will give people the courage to progress beyond external traumas as they occur. Had he been alive today, Maslow would doubtlessly have agreed. Although we might also imagine him taking Enright by the shoulder, sitting him by the fire, and asking him what his thoughts were on transcendence or the growth mindset because, had Enright continued reading, he would have realized that Maslow already had all this covered.

While the pictorial representation of Maslow's theory as a pyramid may be iconic, it is an unhelpful metaphor because typically it is the simplified, five-stage model that is widely represented, particularly in psychology textbooks and the world of business and management courses. In deliberately ignoring the refinements and modifications Maslow made throughout his lifetime, the model being presented is incomplete, and therefore inaccurate, rendering it impossible to test empirically. Furthermore, it continues to encourage the isolation of one need from another and the misconception that they can only be satisfied in ascending order. It is clear throughout Maslow's works that this is not the case but, regardless of how deliberately provocative he became, or how many revisions, corrections and simplifications of his theory he produced to make his intention less ambiguous, misinterpretations and accusations persist.

Those who continue to print, teach and promote his original five-stage model, without any consideration of what Maslow considered to be his magnum opus – the culmination of over 30 years of work – can only be considered negligent. Earlier versions of Maslow's theories are outdated and were only ever intended to get the ball rolling. In death, Maslow's theories – particularly his notions of transcendence – are being dismissed as casually as they were in life, leading Algis Valiunas (2011) to declare: 'How the highest democratic longing—to realize the best in one's nature—has been debased into a pervasive complacency, even a widespread monstrosity, is more than an interesting question in intellectual history; it is a grave and ongoing public catastrophe.'

Transcending current issues surrounding race, gender, poverty, health and religion is our only hope for reversing the narcissistic, self-centred direction in which we are headed, according to Maslow. As far back as 1962 he says:

> *'From Freud we learned that the past exists now in the person. Now we must learn, from growth theory and self-actualization theory that the future also now exists in the person in the form of ideals, hopes, duties,*

tasks, plans, goals, unrealized potentials, mission, fate, destiny, etc. One for whom no future exists is reduced to the concrete, to hopelessness, to emptiness.'

Maslovians Today

Perhaps one of the greatest challenges in describing what we mean by 'Maslovian' is that the man himself was not explicitly focused on one topic or another – rather, he was interested in many psychological and philosophical issues, particularly during what he called his 'post-mortem' life. While the Abramson Family Endowed Fellowship (2005) and the APA's 'Abraham Maslow Award' have been offered to encourage graduate students to carry on the legacy of Maslow, perhaps one of his greatest oversights was failing to monopolize on his graduate students' talents while alive, in order to set into motion some of the ideas he urged others to pursue after his death. His tendency to view them as nothing but nuisances distracting him from his 'calling', now seems a tragic mistake on his part. As a result, more than 50 years later, there are few direct intellectual descendants to Maslow's work.

All the same, his influence lives on through the work of others who have applied Maslow's ideas to their own work. The transpersonal and transhumanistic psychology movements, for example, owe a huge debt to Maslow, one of the founders of the humanistic movement of the 1960s alongside Carl Rogers (1902–1987) and Rollo May (1909–1994). Maslow and Sutich's *Journal of Humanistic Psychology*, established in the Spring of 1961, paved the way for this new area of psychological inquiry and, in 1969, the *Journal of Transpersonal Psychology* was added to the mix. Both journals continue to publish academic papers today, influencing the study of ultimate human capacities including personal growth, spirituality, peak experiences, self-transcendence, and the search for meaning as legitimate topics for academic review.

The work on positive psychology and well-being by American psychologist Martin Seligman (b.1942) can be linked directly back to 'Toward a Positive Psychology', the closing chapter in Maslow's first edition of *Motivation and Personality*. Although Seligman's theories on 'learned helplessness' are innovative, it is clear that the opening statement, 'for the last half century psychology has been consumed with a single topic only – mental illness' in his book *Authentic Happiness* (2002), echoes Maslow's own thoughts from decades before. What is staggering, though, is that Seligman gives no acknowledgement to those, like Maslow, who paved the way before him.

Benedict's concept of synergy became a huge part of Maslow's eupsychian management (eupsychian being the move towards psychological health or self-actualization), his transitional work into Industrial psychology. Despite not receiving the acknowledgement he arguably deserves in his own field, it is difficult to find literature on management that does not pay respect to his contributions. Having observed the effective use of motivation and the move towards peak performance through what he called 'enlightened management' at Non-Linear Systems in California at the invitation of president, Andy Kay in 1962, Maslow's *Eupsychian Management* (now *Maslow on Management*) remains an important standard in organizational management for those applying Maslovian thought into the workplace. Urging organizations to harness the human drive for self-transcendence, his paper 'Theory Z', published in 1969 in the *Journal of Transpersonal Psychology*, foreshadowed the best of Japanese management which rewards employee loyalty through stable employment and paying attention to their morale and general well-being, both on and off the job.

In *The Farther Reaches of Human Nature*, Maslow declares that the greatest advancements we will see in the future will not be focused on ultimate values, but on technology which, he says, he hopes will allow scientists to measure subjective experiences such as the peak and plateau experiences. Using brainwaves, biofeedback and EEG, Maslow claims that 'the mind-body problem appears to be workable after all and scientists should get to solving the problem'. Indeed, the notion that people emerge from a transcendent experience feeling changed and transformed has led to the use of psychedelic drugs such as psyclobin to initiate peak experiences in the treatment of tobacco addiction (Garcia-Romeu et al, 2014) and to reduce symptoms of depression and anxiety in cancer patients, with impressive results (Griffiths et al, 2016). Although Maslow was concerned that peak experiences must not be pursued for hedonistic purposes, as had been the case at Esalen, he would be delighted to know that his work on the effects of the peak experience, regardless of how it is achieved, has led to such positive outcomes.

Unfortunately, what is most closely associated with being Maslovian today is the hierarchy of needs, perhaps the most controversial of all his works. However, if we use his complete eight-stage model to explain the public's emergency reaction to the Covid-19 pandemic (at the time of writing) arguably the most disruptive event in modern history, we can see just how effective it is. Despite the criticism surrounding Maslow's bias towards Western culture, given that the spread of Covid-19 is indiscriminate in terms of its effect on both public health and economies worldwide, the fight against the pandemic has seen all of humanity banding together. As predicted, typical emergency reactions were seen in people regressing from the higher 'being' needs to the more prepotent need for food and shelter further down the hierarchy while others, notably the public healthcare and front-line workers, were transcending the more prepotent safety needs to serve a purpose outside of themselves. Indeed, the astounding surge of volunteers across the UK – a million-strong network – has not reached this level of involvement since WWII. Maslow's notion of transcendence may have been largely ignored by the science community, but the potential exists in all of us. Demonstrating the values that Maslow wished for us might just be the only way we have of showing our gratitude to the man who never wavered in his belief that, as a species, we are inherently good.

Where to Now?

During his tenure as president of the APA in 1968, Maslow was actively involved in the civil rights cause. Seeing racial inequality as one of the great problems of his day he stated that his first objective was to work for greater recognition of black psychologists like Joseph White (1932–2017) due to his belief that the scientific community had deliberately overlooked their achievements and potential contributions to the field of psychology. While disappointed to find that few of his peers viewed this issue as a priority, Maslow resigned himself to the conclusion that they were unlikely to make any special concessions beyond being scrupulously fair. But in April of that same year, in response to the King-assassination riots that led to possibly the greatest wave of social unrest since the American Civil War, Maslow was joined by Rogers and many other leading psychologists to draft a letter to all members highlighting their apprehensions. With a focus on racial prejudice and the resultant discrimination, unemployment and poverty evident across the nation, they warned that the emergent death and destruction would continue to intensify unless the insincere, vague expressions of hope were exchanged with concrete evidence of change with immediate effect.

More than 50 years later, in 2021 at the time of writing, we could argue that this letter never reached its intended destination. It is easy to feel despondent when reading Maslow's excitement in Hoffman's (1999) biography where he says, 'I have a very strong sense of being in the middle of a historical wave. One hundred and fifty years from now, what will historians say about this age?' Despite his warnings, society today appears to be no more civilized than 1960s America. War remains a constant threat across the globe resulting in mass migration of refugees seeking safety and freedom in countries that remain somewhat hostile to their plight. The counterculture of 'turn on, tune in and drop out' is alive and kicking in terms of addiction to pain medication, costing the USA approximately $78.5 billion per year; current rates of lone-parent families standing at 23% in the United States (pewresearch.orgstatista.com) and 21% in the United Kingdom; and a movement of intensely disaffected people of colour are looking towards the BLM (Black Lives Matter) movement to instigate the change that Maslow entrusted to psychologists decades before. Now, more than ever, at such unprecedented times of global turbulence, it would be an act of gross negligence to continue to disregard Maslow's stirring vision of building a psychology for the peace table, perhaps his most prescient vision. We might argue that we are still in a chaos of 'valuelessness' where none of us knows how or what to choose any more than we know how to protect and justify our choices. And yet, Maslow's characteristics of those who self-transcend are emerging from the shadows. People like you. People of all creeds and colour, all of whom Maslow believed to be extraordinary in their own potentialities, are no longer relying on science for immediate change but, instead, are taking personal responsibility and forging a united brotherhood to put Maslow's dreams for humanity into action.

In an interview with *Psychology Today* (1968), Maslow was asked 'If a rare, self-actualizing young psychologist came to you today and said, "What's the most important thing I can do in this time of crisis?", what advice would you give?'. He replied, 'Get to work on aggression and hostility [...] time is running out. A key to understanding the evil which can destroy our society lies in this understanding.'

So, what are you waiting for? According to Maslow, someone must take responsibility and, if not you, then who?

Bibliography

Works by Maslow

Maslow, A.H. (1935). 'Individual psychology and the social behavior of monkeys and apes'. *International Journal of Individual Psychology*, 4, pp.47–59.

Maslow, A.H. (1936). 'The Role of Dominance in the Social and Sexual Behavior of Infra-human Primates (four parts)'. *Journal of Genetic Psychology*, 48: pp.261–338; 49: pp.161–198.

Maslow, A.H. (1943). 'A Theory of Human Motivation'. *Psychological Review*, 50, pp.370–396.

Maslow A.H. (1946). 'Problem-centering vs. Means-centering in Science'. *Philosophy of Science*, 13(4), pp.326– 331.

Maslow A.H. (1950). 'Self-actualizing people: a study of psychological health'. *Personality, Symposium 1*, pp.11–34

Maslow, A.H. (1954). *Motivation and Personality*. New York: Harper Brothers (this edition 1970).

Maslow, A.H. (1961). 'Health as Transcendence of Environment'. *Journal of Humanistic Psychology*, 1(1), pp.1–7. Available at https://doi.org/10.1177/002216786100100102

Maslow, A.H. (1962). *Toward a Psychology of Being*. NY: Van Nostrand.

Maslow, A.H. (1964). *Religions, Values, and Peak-experiences*. Columbus: Ohio State University Press.

Maslow, A.H. (1965a). 'Self-Actualization and Beyond'. U.S. Department of Health, Education & Welfare Office of Education. Retrieved Feb 2022 from https://files.eric.ed.gov/fulltext/ED012056.pdf.

Maslow, A.H. (1965b). *Eupsychian management: A journal.* Homewood, Ill: R.D. Irwin.

Maslow, A.H (1966). *The Psychology of Science: A Reconnaissance.* New York: Harper and Row.

Maslow, A. H. (1967). 'A theory of metamotivation: the biological rooting of the value-life'. *Humanistic Psychology*, 7(2), pp.93–127. Available at https://doi.org/10.1177/002216786700700201.

Maslow, A.H. (1968a). *Toward a Psychology of Being.* New York: Wiley.

Maslow, A.H. (1968b). 'A Conversation with Abraham Maslow'. (E. Hoffman, Interviewer). *Psychology Today.* Retrieved Jan 2022 from https://www.psychologytoday.com/sg/articles/199201/abraham-maslow

Maslow, A.H. & Honigmann, J. (1970). 'Synergy: Some Notes of Ruth Benedict'. *American Anthropologist*, 72(2), new series, pp.320–333. Retrieved 10 April 2021. Available at http://www.jstor.org/stable/671574.

Maslow, A.H. (1971). *The Farther Reaches of Human Nature.* New York: Viking Press.

Maslow, A.H. (1979). *The Journals of A. H. Maslow.* Monterey, CA: Brooks/Cole Publishing.

Maslow, A.H. (1987). *Motivation and Personality.* (3rd ed.). New York, NY: Harper & Row.

Other works cited

Adler, A. (2013). *The Science of Living.* Routledge.

Ansbacher, H.L. & Ansbacher, R.R. (1956) (Eds.) *The Individual Psychology of Alfred Adler: A systematic presentation in selections from his writings.* New York: Basic Books.

Asch, S.E. (1956). 'Studies of independence and conformity: I. A minority of one against a unanimous majority'. *Psychological Monographs: General and Applied, 70*(9), pp.1–70. Available at https://doi.org/10.1037/h0093718.

Babcock, B. (1992). '"Not in the Absolute Singular": Re-Reading Ruth Benedict'. *Frontiers: A Journal of Women Studies, 12*(3), pp.39–77. doi:10.2307/3346643

Banner, Lois. (2003). *Intertwined lives: Margaret Mead, Ruth Benedict, and their circle.* New York: Alfred A. Knopf.

Baumeister, R.F., & Leary, M.R. (1995). 'The Need to Belong: Desire for Interpersonal Attachments as a Fundamental Human Motivation.' *Psychological Bulletin*, pp.97–529.

Brady-Amoon, P. (2012). Maslow, A.H. in: Rieber R.W. (Eds.) *Encyclopedia of the History of Psychological Theories.* Springer, New York, NY

Bridgman, T., Cummings, S., & Ballard, J. (2019). 'Who Built Maslow's Pyramid? A History of the Creation of Management Studies' Most Famous Symbol and Its Implications for Management Education'. *Academy of Management Learning & Education, 18*(1).

Cleary, T.S., & Shapiro, S.I. (1995). 'The plateau experience and the post-mortem life: Abraham H. Maslow's unfinished theory'. *Journal of Transpersonal Psychology, 27*(1), pp.1–23.

Compton, W.C. (2018). 'Self-actualization myths: What did Maslow really say?' *Journal of Humanistic Psychology*, 41, pp.13–29.

DeCarvalho, R.J. (1991). 'The Founders of Humanistic Psychology'. *Thought: Fordham University Quarterly, 66*(1), pp.97–126.

Dye, K., Mills, A.J. & Weatherbee, T. (2005). 'Maslow: Man Interrupted: Reading Management Theory in Context.' *Management Decision 43*(10), pp.1375–1395.

Enright, R.D. (2012). *The Forgiving Life.* American Psychological Association. Washington.

Freud, S. & Strachey, J. (1961). *The Future of an Illusion.* New York: Norton.

Freud, S. (1930). *Civilization and its Discontents.* Ed. by J. Strachey. Sigmund Freud Collection (Library of Congress). (This edn 1962 pub. by W.W. Norton & Co, Inc., NY).

Garcia-Romeu, A., R.R. Griffiths and M.W. Johnson, (2014) 'Psilocybin-Occasioned Mystical Experiences in the Treatment of Tobacco Addiction', *Current Drug Abuse Reviews* 7(157). Available at https://doi.org/10.2174/187 4473708666150107121331.

Geller, L. (1982). 'The Failure of Self-Actualization Theory.' *Journal of Humanistic Psychology,* 22(2), pp.56–73. Available at https://doi.org/10.1177/0022167882222004.

Goldstein, K. (1995). *The Organism: A holistic approach to biology derived from pathological data in man.* NY: Zone Books.

Griffiths, R.R., Johnson, M.W., Carducci, M.A., Umbricht, A., Richards, W.A., Richards, B.D., Cosimano, M.P. & Klinedinst, M.A. (2016). 'Psilocybin produces substantial and sustained decreases in depression and anxiety in patients with life-threatening cancer: A randomized double-blind trial.' *Journal of Psychopharmacology* (Oxford, England), 30(12), pp.1181–1197. Available at https://doi.org/10.1177/0269881116675513.

Haggbloom, S.J., Warnick, R., Warnick, J.E., Jones, V.K., Yarbrough, G.L., Russell, T.M., Borecky, C.M., McGahhey, R., Powell III, J.M., Beavers, J., & Monte, E. (2002). 'The 100 Most Eminent Psychologists of the 20th Century'. *Review of General Psychology,* 6(2), pp.139–152.

Hardeman, M. (1979). 'A Dialogue with Abraham Maslow'. *Journal of Humanistic Psychology,* 19(1), pp.23–28. Available at https://doi.org/10.1177/002216787901900103.

Harlow, H.F. & Zimmermann, R.R. (1958). 'The development of affective responsiveness in infant monkeys'. *Proceedings of the American Philosophical Society,* 102, pp.501–509.

History.com Editors (2010). 'The U.S. Home Front During World War II'. Available at https://www.history.com/topics/world-war-ii/us-home-front-during-world-war-ii.

Hoffman, E. (1992). 'Abraham Maslow. Overcoming Evil: An interview with Abraham Maslow, founder of humanistic psychology'. *Psychology Today*. Retrieved 1 October 2020 from https://www.psychologytoday.com/us/articles/199201/abraham-maslow.

Hoffman, E. (1999). *The Right to be Human: A Biography of Abraham Maslow*. New York, NY: McGraw Hill.

Hoffman, E. (1999). 'Abraham Maslow: A Brief Reminiscence.' In: *Journal of Humanistic Psychology*, *48*(4), pp.443–444.

Kaufman, S.B. (2020). *Transcend: The New Science of Self-Actualization*. New York, NY: Penguin Random House.

Kolbrener, W. (2008). 'Review of Putnam Camp: Sigmund Freud, James Jackson Putnam, and the Purpose of American Psychology'. *Common Knowledge* *14*(1), p.170. Available at https://www.muse.jhu.edu/article/232539.

Kenrick, D.T., Griskevicius, V., Neuberg, S.L., & Schaller, M. (2010). 'Renovating the pyramid of needs: Contemporary extensions built upon ancient foundations.' *Perspectives on Psychological Science*, 5, pp.292–314.

Koltko-Rivera, M.E. (2006). 'Rediscovering the Later Version of Maslow's Hierarchy of Needs: Self-Transcendence and Opportunities for Theory, Research, and Unification'. *Review of General Psychology*, 10, pp.302–317.

Levy D. (1945). 'Psychic trauma of operations in children: and a note on combat neurosis'. *American Journal of Diseases of Children*, 69, pp.7–25.

Mabe A.G., Forney K.J. and Keel P.K. (2014). 'Do you "like" my photo? Facebook use maintains eating disorder risk'. *International Journal of Eating Disorders*; DOI: 10.1002/eat.22254.

McClelland, D. (1964). *The Roots of Consciousness*. New York: Van Nostrand Reinhold.

Money-Kyrle, R.E. (1944). 'Towards a common aim – a psychoanalytical contribution to ethics.' *British Journal of Medical Psychology*, 20, pp.105–117.

Moss, D. (1999). 'Abraham Maslow and the emergence of humanistic psychology'. In: D. Moss, (Ed.). *Humanistic and transpersonal psychology: A historical and biographical sourcebook* (pp.24–34). Westport, CT: Greenwood Press. Retrieved 9 February 2021, from Questia database: http://www.questia.com/PM.qst?a=o&d=54838552.

The National WWII Museum, New Orleans. 'Take A Closer Look: America Goes to War'. Available at https://www.nationalww2museum.org/students-teachers/student-resources/research-starters/america-goes-war-take-closer-look (Accessed 13 April 2021).

Nicholson, Ian (2001). 'Giving up maleness: Abraham Maslow, masculinity, and the boundaries of psychology'. *History of Psychology, 4*(1), pp.79–91.

Odajnyk V.W. (2012) 'Alfred Adler: Extraverted Soulful Physis Eros Type'. In: *Archetype and Character*. Palgrave Macmillan, London. Available at https://doi.org/10.1057/9781137008886_7.

Okech, A. and Chambers, R. (2012), 'Gender Differences in Self-Actualization'. Renée Chambers, C. and Vonshay Sharpe, R. (Eds.) *Black Female Undergraduates on Campus: Successes and Challenges (Diversity in Higher Education, Vol. 12)*, Emerald Group Publishing Limited, Bingley, pp.59–74.

Podeschi, R. (1983). 'Maslow's Dance with Philosophy'. *Journal of Thought, 18*(4), pp.94–100. Retrieved 31 July 2020, from http://www.jstor.org/stable/42589035.

Pow, S. & Stahnisch, F.W. (2014). 'The Organism: A Holistic Approach to Biology Derived from Pathological Data in Man by Kurt Goldstein'. *Journal of the History of the Neurosciences, 23*(3), pp.330–332. DOI: 10.1080/0964704X.2013.860512.

Ryan, B.J., Coppola, D., Canyon, D.V., Brickhouse, M. & Swienton, R. (2020). 'COVID-19 Community Stabilization and Sustainability Framework: An Integration of the Maslow Hierarchy of Needs and Social Determinants of Health'. *Disaster medicine and public health preparedness*, pp.1–7. Advance online publication available at https://doi.org/10.1017/dmp.2020.109.

Saeednia. Y. (2009). 'The need to know and to understand in Maslow's basic needs hierarchy'. *US–China Education Review, 6*(9).

Seligman, M.E.P. (2002). *Authentic Happiness: Using the New Positive Psychology to Realize Your Potential for Lasting Fulfillment.* New York: Free Press.

Suomi, S.J. & Leroy, H.A. (1982). 'In memoriam: Harry F. Harlow (1905–1981)'. *American Journal of Primatology*, 2, pp.319–342.

Sutich, A. (1976). 'The emergence of the transpersonal orientation: A personal account'. *Journal of Transpersonal Psychology*, *8*(1), pp.5–19.

Tay, L., & Diener, E. (2011). 'Needs and subjective well-being around the world'. *Journal of personality and social psychology*, *101*(2), pp.354–65.

Valiunas, A. (2011). "Abraham Maslow and the All-American Self," *The New Atlantis*, No. 33, Fall 2011, pp.93–110. Available at https://www.thenewatlantis.com/publications/abraham-maslow-and-the-all-american-self (Accessed 5 Nov, 2020).

Van Dijken, S., van der Veer, R., van Ljzendoorn, M., & Kuipers, H. J. (1998). 'Bowlby before Bowlby: The sources of an intellectual departure in psychoanalysis and psychology'. *Journal of the History of the Behavioral Sciences*, *34*(3) pp.247–269.

Vitz, P.C. (1994). *Psychology as Religion the Cult of Self-Worship.* Wm. B. Eerdmans Publishing

Wertheimer, M. (1935). 'Some problems in the theory of ethics. In M. Henle (Ed.), *Documents of Gestalt Psychology* (1961), pp.29–41. Berkeley: University of California Press.

Wertheimer, M. (1965). 'Relativity and Gestalt: A Note on Albert Einstein and Max Wertheimer.' *Journal of the History of the Behavioral Sciences*, 1, pp.86–87.

Wilson, C. (1972). *New Pathways in Psychology: Maslow and the Post-Freudian Revolution.* New York: Taplinger.

Wilson, C. (1979). *The Journals of A. H. Maslow.* Monterey, CA: Brooks/Cole Publishing

Zwart, H.A.E. (2019). 'Alfred Adler's Concept of Organ Inferiority.' In: *Purloined Organs.* Palgrave Pivot, Cham. Available at https://doi.org/10.1007/978-3-030-05354-3_11.

Biography

Elizabeth Banks is a Chartered Psychologist with a BSc in Psychology and an MSc in Health Psychology from the University of Kent. After working in the Middle East and Singapore for the past twelve years, Lizzie is now enjoying a sabbatical with her husband, overlanding the USA in a modified Jeep Willy's.

Acknowledgements

To my editor, Alice Bowden, I thank you. Without your keen eye, constant guidance and great sense of humour throughout – who knows what Maslow may have looked like. To my family, thank you for your patience and your uncanny perception of when to leave the office door closed. You now have my undivided attention.

Picture Credits:

Main image: Abraham Maslow. GRANGER - Historical Picture Archive / Alamy Stock Photo **Fig. 1** Brooklyn Public Library, New York. Wikimedia Commons. **Fig. 2** Abe's cousin, Will Maslow, c.1940. American Jewish Congress, Attribution, via Wikimedia Commons. **Fig. 3** The Kanizsa Triangle, via Wikimedia Commons. **Fig. 4** The Rubin Vase, via Wikimedia Commons. **Figs. 5–9** Illustrations copyright Bowden & Brazil Ltd.

Who the hell is

This exciting new series of books sets out to explore the life and theories of the world's leading intellectuals in a clear and understandable way. The series currently includes the following subject areas:

Art History | Psychology | Philosophy | Sociology | Politics

For more information about forthcoming titles in the Who the hell is...? series, go to: **www.whothehellis.co.uk**.

If any of our readers would like to put in a request for a particular intellectual to be included in our series, then please contact us at **info@whothehellis.co.uk**.

Printed in Great Britain
by Amazon

24641108R00078